HIGH FIVE YOUR SPIRIT GUIDES

KATHERINE MARIE

INNER
COMPASS
MEDIA

Published by **Inner Compass Media**

This book is intended for informational and inspirational purposes only. The author is not a licensed medical, legal, or mental health professional, and the content of this book should not be considered a substitute for professional advice. Always seek the guidance of qualified professionals regarding any questions or concerns you may have.

Any references to spiritual practices, intuition, or personal growth reflect the author's experiences and perspectives. Readers are encouraged to use their own discernment and personal judgment when applying any ideas or practices discussed in this book.

This is a work of non-fiction. Names, experiences, and examples are shared with respect for privacy. Any resemblance to actual persons, living or dead, beyond the author's own experiences, is coincidental.

ISBN: 979-8-9921432-1-8

Contents

Introduction

You don't have to believe everything
in this book.

You don't even have to believe anything yet.
Just notice.

That's where connection begins.

1

Soooo... You Found This Book. Let's Acknowledge That

Let's start with a simple truth. People don't pick up a book with the words "spirit guides" in the title by accident. There has to be a reason. Maybe you're curious. Maybe you're hopeful. Maybe you're spiritually hungry but also slightly suspicious of anything too mystical. Or maybe, and my personal favorite, you've had just enough weird things happen in your life that you're starting to think, *"Okay, I don't know what's happening, but something is going on."*

If that's you, grab a stool. You are in the right place.

Because here's the thing nobody tells you. You're not crazy for wondering if something is nudging you, helping you, guiding you, or trying to get your attention. In fact, you're in excellent company. Great thinkers, scientists, artists, and everyday people throughout history have all felt that quiet hum of connection. And now you're here, holding a book that's going to help you make sense of it. The best part? There's no pressure. No heavy doctrine. No weird robes. Just you, me, and a growing awareness that you're not wandering through life alone.

Two Kinds of Readers Arrive Here

I'm guessing that there are two kinds of readers who open this book, and they tend to fall into either of these groups:

Group One: "I believe in something… I just don't know what." These readers have stories they don't usually talk about but definitely can't stop thinking about. Such as that time they followed a sudden urge and avoided something bad, or the dream that felt more like a message, or the coincidence that was a little too precise to be random. They're open, curious, and ready to learn more.

Group Two: "Okay, I'm curious, but don't make it weird." These readers want to believe, but they're cautious. They're skeptical in a healthy, grounded way. They're not here for magical thinking or the woo woo. They want something that feels real, accessible, and not embarrassing to describe to a friend at brunch.

Whichever group you belong to, you're exactly where you need to be. And yes, you can switch between the two. I certainly have.

Let's Clear the Air About Doubt

If you're thinking: *"What if I'm making all this up?"* or *"I love the idea of spirit guides but I'm afraid to fully believe."* That's great. Really. That means you're paying attention. This isn't a book that demands belief. This is a book that asks for openness. There is a big difference between the two. You don't have to take a giant leap of faith here. You just need to consider the possibility that the same intelligence that guides the stars might also be whispering to *you.*

That's it.

A Quick Gut-Check Exercise

Before we go any further, let's get you involved. Right now, grab something to write on. A notebook, an envelope, a napkin, the back of a grocery receipt… anything. Now, write down three times in your life when you followed your gut. Moments where something inside you said *this way*, and you listened. Then, write down three times you ignored your gut and wished later you hadn't. Don't overthink it. Take all the time you need. Simply jot down what comes to mind. It can be huge or small. This exercise isn't about judgment. It's about showing you, with your own memories, that you've already been guided in ways you didn't recognize.

Now, look at your list. Here's what you're going to notice. One, when you followed your gut, things usually worked out or saved you trouble. And two, when you didn't follow your gut, you often paid for it. That inner voice? That pull? That intuitive nudge you brushed off? That's the channel we're going to strengthen in this book. You've already experienced guidance. Now we're going to help you understand it.

And don't worry. You won't need to stop and scramble for supplies every time an exercise comes up. All the exercises in this book are collected again in one easy section at the back, so you can revisit them anytime, at your own pace, whenever it feels right.

You're Not Starting from Zero

Even if you've never meditated, never used a pendulum, never pulled a tarot card, and don't consider yourself "intuitive," you're still not a beginner. Humans come factory-installed with intuition. Spirit guides don't have to suddenly "appear." They've been whispering all along. You're simply learning to hear them on purpose. Think of this chapter as the moment you pull the dusty chain on the overhead light in a room you've been standing in your whole life. The room didn't change. You simply finally saw it.

Where We're Going from Here

In the next chapter, I'll share how I wound up on this path. Not because my story is more special than anyone else's, but because it shows that you don't need mystical credentials to start a spiritual partnership with your guides. But for now? Sit with what you wrote. Let those memories remind you that the mysterious isn't foreign, it's familiar. You're already in conversation with the universe. You're simply learning to speak the language.

Reflection for the End of Chapter One

Before you turn the page, take a quiet moment and ask yourself one simple question: "What part of me is hoping this is real?" You don't need to write it down. Don't justify anything. Just… notice.

Is it the part of you that's tired of doing life alone? The part that feels something bigger has been nudging you? The part that's secretly relieved this book exists? Or maybe it's the part that's finally ready to believe in a deeper connection? Sit with whatever comes up, even if it's only a whisper. Your answer is the doorway we'll walk through in the next chapter.

2

Why Me? Trust Me, I Asked the Same Thing

Let me start with one key fact: I'm not a mystic. I'm not an oracle, a psychic medium, a clairvoyant, or someone who wakes up in the morning with messages from the universe. If you're imagining me sitting cross-legged in a robe, chanting at dawn… that is adorable, but wildly inaccurate.

I'm just me. A regular person who didn't have the credentials for any of this, and who still sometimes looks over my shoulder and whispers, "Are you sure I'm the one who should be doing this?" But that's exactly why you can trust me. Because if someone like me can connect with their spirit guides, deepen that relationship, and maybe write a book about it, then absolutely anyone can. Including you.

Childhood Whispers (Also Known as "Imaginary Friends")

Growing up, I had an "imaginary friend." At the time, I'm sure everyone thought it was cute, normal kid stuff. And it was, except looking back? I don't think that friend was really all that imaginary. A beautiful truth is, kids don't second-guess magic. They don't demand data and peer-reviewed studies. They simply know what they feel, and as a kid, I felt someone with me. Always. It was my first spirit guide, though I didn't have that language yet. Somewhere between childhood and paying my first taxes, that sense dulled. Not because my spirit guides got quiet, but because adulthood got loud. Still, even then, guidance never fully left. I was always someone with "good instincts."

Don't get me wrong. I made some impressively terrible decisions too. Real "oh honey, no" choices. I'm sure my spirit guides were pacing in the background, stress-eating celestial popcorn and yelling at the ceiling. But somehow, all roads, good and disastrous, still led me exactly where I'm supposed to be right now. Sitting here writing this book for both of us.

Let's Get This Out of the Way: No Titanic Moments

Let me be clear. I don't have a dramatic "the spirit guides saved my life" moment to point to. No last-minute decision that spared me from ultimate disaster. Alas, no lottery win (but I still hold out hope on that one). No fortune cookie delivering cryptic instructions. What I do have are hundreds of little whispers that steered me, protected me, or shoved me toward something good. Little intuitive nudges, sudden gut feelings, and ideas that came out of nowhere. Moments where I listened to that tiny voice… and it changed something. And honestly? There are probably near-misses and cosmic interventions I'll never even know about.

Pause Here: A Quick Warm-Up Exercise

(Don't skip this, it's a fun one.) Think about your life for a second. Who was your imaginary friend? Or the source of your creative ideas, work breakthroughs, sudden solutions, or late-night inspired thoughts? Everyone has one, even if they don't call it a spirit guide.

Grab your notebook or your phone, or wherever you want to write stuff, and jot down:

1. A moment when you felt "guided" in a creative or problem-solving way.
2. A moment when you felt an idea suddenly appear.
3. A moment when something worked out and you thought, "Huh… that was weirdly perfect timing."

Your spirit guides have been whispering to you for years. You're finally starting to notice.

The Quiet Truth: I Was Always Guided

Even when I didn't believe in anything, even when I thought intuition was only "a feeling" or even when I rolled my eyes at anything that seemed too mystical, the nudges were still there. Looking back, I see many, many times something, or someone, helped to steer me. Like the sudden urge to turn left instead of right, the unexpected perfect idea that came out of nowhere, or the job opportunity that appeared exactly when I needed it. I simply didn't realize these were my spirit guides, tapping me on the shoulder. Once you start paying attention, you'll see you've had these moments, too.

The Last Year Changed Everything

I didn't wake up one day able to talk to spirit guides as if I was tuning into a celestial podcast. This past year was one of learning, unlearning, experimenting, doubting, trying again, and finally, well I guess the word would be, *opening.* I went to talks and classes about connecting with the higher self, including one specifically on spirit guides. I went to a retreat in the Washington woods, whereby the end of the three days they pegged me as The Storyteller. That label hit me right in the soul, because it was exactly what I'd always been. But the real ignition moment?

That was Sedona.

Sedona: Where the Red Rocks Whispered

Sedona is one of those places where the sky feels wider and the ground hums under your feet. People call it a vortex area. I call it… a very good decision. It was really nothing more than a pit stop on a two-week road trip between Portland and Tucson. Yet, in a small crystal shop, I saw a sign offering tarot readings. Now, the only "tarot readings" I'd had up to that point involved messing around with friends, wine, and questionable decision-making. The reading was pricey, so I shrugged it off. Yet, the idea followed me for an entire day of hiking among those massive red rocks and so the next night, before leaving town, I went back.

The reading wasn't theatrical or dramatic, but it was clear. I was going to write a book. Something unlike anything I'd written before. Something from my soul. I didn't believe it at the time. Who was I to write a spiritual book? Me? A person who couldn't even meditate for more than twelve seconds? So I tucked it away as a "cool Sedona moment." But the seed was planted. And spirit guides? Trust me, they are excellent gardeners.

I Didn't Choose the Topic—It Chose Me

I can't pinpoint the exact moment I knew I was writing this book. There wasn't a bolt of lightning. No giant neon sign in the sky. There was only a feeling. Like breadcrumbs, or nudges, and a sense of rightness every time I imagined helping people find their spirit guides the way I found mine.

Then one morning over breakfast with my partner, out of nowhere, I blurted, "I'm going to write a book about spirit guides." Not "someday." Not "I might." Simply… I'm writing it. And the title? That came to me in one perfect mental snapshot of my spirit guides, high-fiving each other as if they were a baseball team that had just won the championship. I swear they were celebrating when I finally acknowledged this guidebook needed to be written. And honestly? I think they still are. They're also hovering around my laptop right now, reading this over my shoulder. (Yes, I know that makes me sound slightly bananas. You'll get used to it.)

Tarot, Pendulums, Crystals… Oh My

Since that Sedona trip, I've gone all-in on learning the language of intuition. Tarot cards? Love them. Pendulum work? New to me, but I use mine every day now. Crystals? Oh, I have them. All of them. Enough to require a shelving intervention. Candles? Stockpiled as if I'm preparing for a mystical blackout. And if you're picturing candles and crystals glowing around my laptop right now, you're absolutely correct. More importantly, I'm learning, practicing, and growing every day. Not because I'm special and not because I'm gifted, but because I'm open. And you're here because some part of you is ready to open too.

Try This: A Simple Question with a Big Answer

This is your chance to pause, not for long, but long enough to actually feel something open. Wherever you are right now, take a breath. Let your body relax. Let your mind unclench a little. Now write the answer to this: "When in my life did I feel something was guiding me, even if I didn't know what it was?" Don't overthink it. Don't scroll through your entire life like you're searching old photos. Don't try to find the "most spiritual" moment. Notice the first memory that rises.

It might be a near miss, a strange coincidence, a perfectly timed opportunity, or meeting someone who showed up out of nowhere and changed your life. It doesn't need to be dramatic or mystical. It simply needs to feel as if something or someone had your back. Once you've written that moment down, reflect on it. Why that moment? Why did that memory, of all things, surface first out of everything that has happened in your life? Did you brush it off at the time? Did you tell yourself it was nothing? Coincidence? Luck?

How does that moment feel now, reading this book? Does it feel different? More meaningful? More connected? Sit with your answers for a few seconds. This memory is not random. It's your intuition showing you the doorway you've already walked through once… maybe more than once. And now? You're going to walk through it on purpose.

So, Seriously... Why Me? Because I'm Walking This Path the Same Way You Are

I'm guessing you don't want a guru on a mountaintop writing this book. You want someone like you. Someone who wondered "Is this real? Or am I just imagining things?" Someone who said, "Even if I'm not ready, maybe it's time to begin." That's why this chapter is called "Why Me?" and not "Why I Was Chosen by the Glowing Spirits of the Fifth Dimension." Because I wasn't chosen. I simply said yes. And now? You're saying yes, too. You know what I think? I think your spirit guides are high-fiving each other right now because they've been waiting for this moment, maybe for your whole life. And in Chapter Three, we're going to talk about who they are and what they've been trying to show you all along.

3

The Team You Didn't Know You Had

When it comes to spirit guides, I think of it as each of us coming into this life with our own cosmic superhero team assigned at birth. Not the cape-wearing, spandex kind, although honestly, if that visual helps, run with it. These spirit guides don't have bodies or form. They're pure energy, but not the vague, hard-to-grasp "floaty" kind. Think of them as the energetic equivalent of the best support squad you've ever had. Like superheroes, they can do things we can't. Fly, slip through walls, multitask without caffeine, appear everywhere at once, all without breaking a sweat. They're always with us. Sometimes it's only one. Sometimes there's a whole crew. They tap in and out depending on what we are facing, the same way specialists step in on a team when their skill is needed.

Their purpose? Our greater good, our higher path, and our growth. Their main job is to nudge us toward alignment and help us get what we really want. Best of all, they never, ever get angry, frustrated, or disappointed in us. Spirit guides don't judge. They don't roll their eyes when you make a questionable life choice. They follow us into every situation, even the ones where the soundtrack probably should've warned us, "Girl… don't do it." They don't lie. They don't manipulate. They don't lead us astray. Their entire operating system runs on positivity, truth, clarity, and support.

For most of my life, my spirit guides weren't "beings." They were more of a feeling, a nudge, a wave of comfort, or a quiet emotional presence that didn't come with a face or a voice. They were similar to trying to describe love. Not the actions of love, just the essence of it. That's what spirit guides feel like: something that simply *is.* In the last year, though, they've come forward in a more recognizable way. A little more distinct, and a little more interactive. These days, you guessed it, I can even high-five them, which I know isn't everyone's experience, but that's the thing. Spirit guides will meet you in whatever way you naturally connect. They don't need you to see them a certain way. They'll show up in the form, feeling, or personality that feels right to you. Because at their core, spirit guides are exactly the supportive, non-judgmental energy you need to walk beside you, no matter what paths you take.

What Spirit Guides Are Not

Before we go any deeper, let's clear away a few misconceptions. Spirit guides are powerful, supportive, and sometimes surprisingly humorous energies, but they are not a lot of the things people fear or imagine. Here are a few important distinctions.

They are not ghosts. Let's get this one out of the way early. Spirit guides are not apparitions. You will never wake up in the middle of the night with a spirit guide rattling chains or whispering your name from a dark corner as if they're auditioning for a horror movie. They aren't wandering souls who didn't cross over, and they aren't stuck in some cosmic waiting room trying to grab your attention. Spirit guides are not "the dead." They're not lost and are not lingering around you because they have unfinished business.

Your spirit guides are intentional, positive presences that operate from a completely different energetic plane. They come in with purpose, clarity, and a direct connection to your higher path. Not because they're roaming around looking for company. If you've ever been nervous that "connecting to spirit guides" sounds like summoning ghosts… breathe easy. This is not that.

They are not dependent on rituals, tools, or perfect conditions. You don't need incense, chanting, moon phases, a fancy altar, or a spotless house to connect with your spirit guides. They don't require candles, crystals, sage, bowls, bells, or a robe you only wear on solstices. All those things can help focus your energy, and I'll talk more about that later, but spirit guides themselves don't need any of it. They tune into you, not your environment. You can connect with them while folding laundry, writing a book, sitting in traffic, or brushing your teeth. They don't need a ritual to reach you because they are already with you. Tools can help you get centered but are never required.

They are never something to fear. This one matters. Spirit guides do not operate from fear, intimidation, or threat. They don't use fear to get your attention, don't scare you to teach lessons, and they absolutely don't create dread or heaviness. The energy of a true spirit guide is always calm, positive, and steady, even when they're nudging you toward a tough truth. If you ever feel afraid while exploring spiritual connection, that fear is coming from inside you. It stems from old programming, uncertainty, or the discomfort of expanding into something new.

But spirit guides themselves? Their frequency is the opposite of fear. Their presence is soft, safe, grounding, and steady. Think "warm hand on your back," not "dark figure in the hallway." You do not need to be afraid of your team. Ever.

They are not one-size-fits-all. If there's one universal truth about spirit guides, it's that everyone experiences them differently. Some people sense them as warmth, while others feel a presence in the room. Some see symbols, images, or patterns right out of the gate, but others feel nothing for years, and then suddenly… everything clicks. There is no "correct" way to connect. Spirit guides show up in the form that feels natural to you. They adapt to your personality, your sensitivities, your life experience, and the way your inner world works. My spirit guides feel a little human to me these days. Accessible, humorous, and high-five-able, but yours may feel subtle, symbolic, or purely energetic. All of it is valid. There is no template or standard model. No universal experience. It's beautiful, and intentionally personal.

A Quick Check-In with Your Cosmic Team

Before you go any further, let's pause for a moment of gentle connection. Nothing dramatic. No incense or chanting required. This is simply a chance to give your energy a moment to recognize what's already around you. Find a comfortable spot, take a slow breath, and ask yourself this one quiet question: "If one of my spirit guides wanted to make themselves known right now, what is the very first feeling, image, or sensation that comes to mind?"

Don't overthink it. Don't analyze it. Don't wait for something big or cinematic. Simply notice whatever shows up first. Maybe a warmth in your chest, or a subtle presence behind your shoulder, or a color. It can be as simple as a word popping into your head or a full-blown memory. Or even simply a sense of something or someone there. It doesn't matter how faint or how unexpected it is. Your spirit guides don't announce themselves with trumpets. They usually show up in the smallest, quietest ways.

Now place a hand over your heart or your stomach, whichever feels more natural, and ask one more simple question: "What do I most need to hear right now?" Again, take the very first thing that rises. A word, a phrase, a feeling, or even simply a sense of reassurance you didn't realize you needed. Don't judge it or filter it. This is how connection begins. Not with lightning bolts, but with subtle awareness and the quiet recognition that you are not alone and never have been.

Other Beings You May Hear About (and How They Fit In)

We've talked about your personal spirit guides, your cosmic superhero team, so let's address the other spiritual beings people love to toss into the mix. Because the moment you say "spirit guides," someone inevitably asks, "But what about angels? And ancestors? And spirit animals? And ascended masters? And my neighbor's cousin who swears she's connected to Archangel Michael?"

Okay, we're going to make this simple. Your spirit guides are your core team. These other beings are more like specialists who may or may not swing by depending on what you need. Let's unpack them without melting your brain.

Ancestors: The Emotional Support Crew

Ancestors are the easiest to understand because they come with built-in familiarity. They're comforting, grounding, and show up when you need a sense of belonging or when your heart needs a hug from someone who "gets" your family line. But here's the thing. They are not your full-time spirit guides. Instead, they pop in when needed, bringing love but not lifelong assignments. Think of them as spiritual drop-in visitors who bring casserole and reassurance.

Angels: The High-Frequency Backup Team

Angels are the beings who show up with big, gentle, protective energy. And no, you don't need to be religious to acknowledge them. A few things to keep straight. One, they're not assigned to a single person. Two, they step in when comfort, clarity, or protection is needed. And three, they're basically the cosmic equivalent of calling customer support and somehow getting the most patient person on earth. Your spirit guides walk with you every day. Angels show up when the moment calls for a little extra light.

Spirit Animals: Symbol, Not Pet

As adorable as it sounds, spirit animals are not astral pets walking alongside you at the end of some cosmic leash. Spirit animals are symbolic messengers and guides that show up through dreams, synchronicities, or repeated signs.

Some people have powerful experiences with their spirit animals. Some don't notice them at all. Both are valid. Most people meet several throughout their lifetime, depending on what they're working through, but again, they are temporary. Need an example? I notice hawks. All the time. They can be the tiniest speck sitting on a light pole, but my eyes are drawn there. Some live in the trees around my house. Coincidence? I don't think so. A lot of people see hummingbirds or crows or butterflies. The list is endless. But they're not full-time members of your team, and instead they're more like, "Heads up. Pay attention. Here's the lesson you need right now. Good luck. Stay hydrated."

Archangels: The Heavy Hitters

These are the big ones. They are the spiritual powerhouses with impressive glowing résumés. Here's all you need to know. They are massive, powerful beings of light. People call on them intentionally, (they don't just drop by for coffee) and they are never your personal spirit guides. They're similar to high-level consultants who are incredible to work with, but not necessary for daily life.

Ascended Masters: The Spiritual Professors

These are figures such as Buddha or Jesus who mastered human life to the point that they basically unlocked the final level. You don't have to feel connected to them (I personally do not, at least not at the moment) and your spirit guide practice is completely valid without them. They're part of the spiritual world's extended universe and important enough to note here.

So how do you make sense of all of this? It's simple. Your spirit guides are your core team. Everyone else is optional support. Take what resonates and leave the rest. You do not need ancestors, angels, spirit animals, archangels, or ascended masters to have a powerful, meaningful, everyday relationship with your spirit guides. Your team is already complete.

A Quick Manifesting Warm-Up with Your Spirit Guides

By now you know your spirit guides are here for your highest good, cheering you on like the cosmic superheroes they are. So let's give you a tiny taste of how manifestation and spirit guides work together. Think of it as an appetizer before the full-course meal later in the book. This exercise is simple, quick, and surprisingly powerful.

Start by sitting comfortably, taking one slow, deep breath, and letting your body relax. You don't need to meditate. You don't need a candle. Simply breathe. Now bring one small desire to mind. Don't go overboard and reach for the beach house, a soulmate, or a million dollars. Begin with a starter desire. Something such as, "I want clarity on a decision," or "I want help finishing a project," or "I want inspiration." Make it simple, manageable, and something you'd be pleasantly surprised to see unfold. Once you have it, say silently or out loud these two sentences:

"Spirit Guides, help me move toward this in the clearest and simplest way. Show me what I need to do and help me notice when you are guiding me."

Now here's the important part. Pay attention to the very next nudge, idea, or feeling that rises. It might feel similar to a gentle tug in the direction of something, an idea popping in that feels oddly obvious, or even a simple sense of yes or no. Write whatever comes up, even if it seems ridiculously small or anticlimactic. Your spirit guides don't drop grand manifestations from the sky like vending-machine snacks. They start with the next breadcrumb, the next step, because manifestation is a co-creation, not a magic trick. And here's the treat… you manifested. Not the end result necessarily, but the beginning of movement toward it.

That's how it works. Your intention, their guidance, and one small shift you can follow through on. You'll learn more about this later, but for now, celebrate that you and your spirit guides just did your first manifesting together. Trust me, the more you do this, the stronger it gets. And next, we're going to talk about how this guidance shows up in everyday life, often in ways so subtle you might miss them if you're not paying attention. Because now that you know who your team is, it's time to learn how they get your attention.

4

Mixed Signals: How & Why We Accidentally Confuse Our Guides

Here's a universal truth your spirit guides already know. Humans are fully capable of wanting something with their whole being and simultaneously slamming the energetic door in its face. It's impressive, honestly. Olympic-level emotional gymnastics. You ask for clarity… then immediately get overwhelmed when a whisper of intuition shows up. You ask for a sign… then dismiss it because surely your spirit guides wouldn't use something that obvious. You ask for courage… then politely tell every courageous impulse to sit down because "now isn't a good time."

Energetic resistance isn't stubbornness. It's self-protection wearing a cute disguise. It's the part of you that craves the new but clings to the old because the old feels safer even if it's boring, cramped, or mildly soul-suffocating. Your spirit guides don't judge this. They've seen it ten thousand times, but from their perspective, it looks a little along the lines of this:

You: "Please bring me an opportunity!"

Spirit Guides: slides the opportunity across the table

You: gasps and pushes it back, "NOT LIKE THAT."

That wobble, that "yes but also no," creates static in the line. Not enough to shut down the connection, but enough to make your spirit guides tilt their heads and wonder, "Are we going forward? Or sideways? Do we need snacks for this?"

Energetic resistance isn't failure. It's only a signal that something inside you wants the thing but doesn't feel ready to receive it. The magic trick is simply noticing when your energy flinches while your words say, "I'm ready." Once you spot that moment, the tiny recoil, you can soften it. You don't have to bulldoze through it or shame yourself for it. Just breathe, acknowledge the fear, and let your spirit guides know that you're a little scared, but they can keep going, because you're still listening. They hear that and suddenly the static clears, the line smooths out, and the whole conversation gets easier.

The "Fear of Success" vs. "Fear of Change" Tangle

Before we dive in, let me clear up one thing. We're not talking about fear of failure here. Most people assume that's their problem. Thoughts along the lines of "It might not work, I might mess it up, or people might judge me" are all fear of failure. Totally normal, but that's not the flavor we're dealing with in this chapter. Fear of success is different. Fear of success says, "What if this does work? What if I have to grow into someone bigger? What if my life changes in ways I can't predict?"

Then there's fear of change, which is its own beast entirely, and comes with "I want things to get better, but I also want everything to stay the same, thanks." These two together create more mixed signals than fear of failure ever does. Think of it as fear of failure slows you down. Fear of success plus fear of change puts you in full energetic whiplash. "Yes, please help me," immediately followed by "WAIT, NOT LIKE THAT."

And your spirit guides? They're watching you pace as if you are a cat who begged to go outside and then immediately panicked the second the door opened. You say you want the breakthrough, the opportunity, and the deeper connection to your spirit guides, but when the energy actually starts moving, you clutch the doorway as if it's the last safe plank on a sinking ship. This is normal. So normal it might as well be a human birthright.

This tangled fear shows up in tiny, subtle ways. How about second-guessing intuitive nudges? Do you ever ask for signs and then declare they "don't count?" Or find yourself "too busy" to meditate or listen? It's all the same dance. The desire to evolve while doing a slow tango with the instinct to stay safe. But here's the beautiful part. Your spirit guides already know the version of you that exists on the other side of these fears. They see the confident, expanded, and grounded you. They're not pushing you. They're inviting you. You don't have to slay the fear. You don't have to become fearless. You simply have to become willing, because willingness melts the tangle. Willingness tells your spirit guides that yes, you are nervous, but you want them to keep guiding you and helping you get what you want.

Quick Check-In: What Fear Is Actually Showing Up?

Take a breath and place a hand over your heart (or right in the center of your upper belly, where your "intuition butterflies" live) and think of something you're trying to call into your life right now. A new opportunity. A creative idea. A deeper connection with your purpose. Whatever pops up first is the right one.

Now read these three prompts slowly and notice which one makes your body clench the most:

1. Fear of Failure

"What if I try and it doesn't work?"

If this one hits home, you'll feel a tightening sensation. A sinking, a contraction, or an "I'm not good enough" wobble.

2. Fear of Success

"What if this actually works and I have to show up bigger than I ever have before?"

This one feels similar to excitement and dread braided together. A thrill with a tiny side of nausea.

3. Fear of Change

"What if this shifts things in ways I can't control?"

This one usually brings up hesitation, overthinking, and the quiet desire to crawl into a blanket fort until further notice.

Whichever prompt made your insides do the most dramatic flip-flop, that's your fear du jour. Don't judge it. Don't fix it. Just name it, because naming untangles everything, and now that you know your fear, you're free to file it away and carry on.

How Spirit Guides Interpret Energy, Not Words

Here's something your spirit guides wish they could gently and lovingly tattoo on your forehead. They don't hear what you say. They hear what you mean. What you mean is conveyed through your energy, not your vocabulary. You can say all the right things out loud. Write gorgeous affirmations in your journal. Light candles, chant mantras, and present your manifestations like a PowerPoint deck to the universe, but if your energy is quietly muttering, "Please no, I'm terrified. Actually, never mind," your spirit guides are going to respond to that.

Think of it as talking to someone who's smiling politely while radiating pure panic. They're nodding and saying, "I'm fine," but their energy is screaming, "This is a hostage situation!" Your spirit guides pick up the scream, not the smile. Humans rely on words because we learn language before we learn intuition. Spirit guides rely on energy because… well… they're spirit guides. Whole different operating system.

When you ask for something, but your energetic field is tight, scared, hesitant, or bracing for impact, your spirit guides don't hear the request as a clear "yes." They hear mixed signals, ambivalence, fear, or "I want it, but I'm not emotionally available for it yet." This is why a single moment of clarity, something as simple as a deep breath with a tiny inner "okay, I'm open," is louder to your spirit guides than an hour of beautifully worded intentions. You can't trick your spirit guides with poetic phrasing. (They appreciate the effort, though.) You can communicate clearly by letting your energy match your request. This doesn't mean being perfect. It means being honest. Sometimes the cleanest message you can send them is: "I want this, and I'm scared, but I'm willing." Energy-wise, that reads as a full-body yes, and your spirit guides light up because they finally have something they can actually work with.

Getting Out of Your Own Way

At some point on the spiritual path, you discover the plot twist no one warns you about. You're not fighting your spirit guides. You're fighting yourself. And honestly, you put up a remarkably strong defense. If self-sabotage were a martial art, you'd have a black belt and a trophy wall.

Getting out of your own way isn't about becoming fearless or disciplined or suddenly enlightened. It's much simpler and much messier. It's about noticing the exact moment you start blocking the very thing you asked for. You know the moments. When intuition whispers a next step and you respond by reorganizing your sock drawer. When you get a crystal-clear sign and suddenly decide you need "just one more sign." When guidance nudges you toward something meaningful and you hide behind a to-do list as if it's a riot shield. This is the human condition.

We crave movement and then cling to stillness because movement feels risky. Your spirit guides see this with so much compassion. They know your desire is real. They also see the panic button you keep under the table.

Getting out of your own way isn't an act of bravery. It's an act of honesty. It means admitting that you're scared but want to keep going. Your comfort zone is cozy, but you can step out for five minutes at a time. The second you allow even a sliver of willingness, the whole energetic landscape shifts. Your spirit guides step forward. Your intuition gets louder. Opportunities line up as if they've been waiting at the door for weeks.

Because here's the secret. You don't have to bulldoze anything. You simply have to stop being the primary obstacle. Getting out of your own way is taking the next step, not the perfect one. It's giving your spirit guides room to respond. When you stop gripping the steering wheel of your life like you're on a roller coaster with faulty brakes, something magical happens. Your spirit guides can finally… guide. Funny how that works. Every time you choose a single moment of openness, you're essentially telling them you're okay. You're still willing. Keep going.

Let's Try Something: The One-Sentence Request Reset

Grab a pen and your journal or whatever you're writing on. We're about to strip your intention down to its cleanest version.

Step 1: Choose one thing you want guidance on. Only one. Not the whole life overhaul. Not the five-year plan. One thing. Big or small. Whatever rises to the surface first.

Step 2: Write the request the way your mind wants to phrase it. Total brain dump. Let it be messy, wordy, dramatic, over-explained… your mind loves a run-on sentence. Let it have its moment.

Step 3: Now rewrite it using only these rules: one sentence, no explanations, no caveats, and no "buts," "ifs," or "as long as." State what you want as clearly and simply as possible.

For example, here's a messy version: *I want clarity about my next step in my career, but I'm scared of making the wrong decision, and I don't want anything too disruptive, and can you show me what's right without shaking my whole life up?"*

And the clean version: "*Show me the next right step.*"

Step 4: Read your one-sentence request out loud. Feel the difference. Your spirit guides hear this far more clearly than the mental monologue version.

Step 5: Add this tiny closing line (it's optional, but wildly effective). *"I'm willing to receive this guidance."* That last part opens the energetic window. You don't have to fling it wide, just crack it open. Your spirit guides can work with a crack better than a locked door.

Why This Exercise Works

Clean requests aren't simply tidy, they're powerful.

Your spirit guides aren't listening for the prettiest words or the most poetic phrasing. They're listening for the core frequency beneath your intention. When your request is cluttered with explanations, fears, and disclaimers, the energetic signal gets buried under emotional static. What this exercise does is strip all that noise away. When you force your intention into a single sentence, your energy gains focus. Instead of sending out six different mini-signals, you're sending one clear one. Your request becomes specific. Your spirit guides love specificity.

When you speak a one-sentence request out loud, your energy aligns behind it. Your whole system organizes around that one desire, and your spirit guides finally get a clean, consistent signal to work with. And when you add, *"I'm willing to receive this guidance,"* you shift from passive asking to active openness. That single line turns your request from a wish into a powerful channel.

Simple Ways to Stop Sending Mixed Messages

By now, you've seen how easy it is to accidentally confuse your spirit guides. Honestly, it's a wonder they don't carry tiny celestial whiteboards to keep track of our mood swings. The good news? Clearing up your energetic communication doesn't require a full spiritual makeover.

You don't need to meditate for three hours, fast for a week, or climb a mountain to whisper your intentions into the wind. Small, simple shifts work beautifully. Here are a few that instantly clean up your signal:

1. Pick one thing at a time. Your spirit guides are brilliant, not psychic project managers juggling twelve competing priorities. Choose one intention you want clarity on. One. This instantly sharpens the message.

2. Say what you want, not what you fear. Your energy

broadcasts the dominant feeling, not the prettiest sentence. If your request is wrapped in anxiety, scarcity, or panic, your spirit guides receive the panic, not the request. Shift from saying you don't want to mess up to please help me take the next right step. Completely different signal.

3. Relax your body before you ask. Spirit guides respond to openness, not tension. Take five seconds and do something gentle. Unclench your jaw, relax your shoulders, soften your belly, and breathe in and out once like you mean it.

4. Ask for guidance you can recognize. Spirit guides love clarity almost as much as they love enthusiasm. It's absolutely okay to ask for a sign you can easily understand or for one that is obvious. Your spirit guides don't think "obvious" is cheating. They think it's helpful.

5. Follow the first nudge. The very first intuitive whisper is almost always the clearest. Everything after that is you negotiating. You know that impulse that pops up before your brain starts holding committee meetings about it? That's the one to follow. Don't worry about being perfect, and focus on what's clear.

6. Acknowledge the guidance you DO receive. Even if you're not sure, even if it's tiny, your spirit guides don't need a parade. They need a nod. A simple thank you is more than enough. It strengthens the channel more than any ritual you could perform. It tells them you're listening, which makes them go, "Great! Let's send more."

Bringing It All Together

Your spirit guides aren't keeping score. They're not frustrated when your signals get glitchy or when you panic about the very things you asked for. They simply adjust, stay patient, and wait for you to relax enough to let the connection clear. Mixed signals aren't a flaw. They're a sign you're growing, stretching, and brushing up against parts of yourself that are waking up. Every time you relax, breathe, get honest, and choose a cleaner request, you shift from confusion to alignment. Just one moment at a time. One clear step. One clean signal. Your spirit guides are already tuned in. Now you're learning to tune in yourself.

Once you understand how easily mixed signals happen, the next natural question is this: how do your spirit guides actually respond when the line clears? Because once you relax, get honest, and stop tripping over your own energy, guidance doesn't arrive as thunderbolts or booming voices. It shows up quietly, casually, and almost sneakily. Through signs, nudges, coincidences, and those little "wait, that felt intentional" moments that are easy to brush off if you're not paying attention. In the next chapter, we're going to talk about exactly how your spirit guides get your attention in the real world and how to start recognizing their cosmic winks when they happen.

5

Signs, Nudges, and Cosmic Winks

Have you ever had one of those moments where something tugs lightly at your awareness, soft as a whisper, and you brush it off… only to have it show up again a little louder? Maybe it's a song on repeat, or a number pattern, or a random thought that refuses to be ignored. That's the language of your spirit guides. Not thunderbolts, not neon arrows pointing from the sky, just quiet and consistent communication.

Your spirit guides love signs because they're the easiest way to slip through the cracks of your everyday life. Signs let them nudge you, comfort you, course-correct you, and occasionally smack you lovingly upside the head when you miss the gentle version. And spoiler: everyone misses the gentle version sometimes. Yes, even me.

Here's the secret most people overlook. Signs aren't rare. Awareness is. Once you start paying attention, you realize your spirit guides have been waving at you for ages. You simply didn't know which wave was for you.

Subtle vs. Obvious Signs

Spirit guides tend to use a sliding scale of communication. Think of it as low-volume to blowhorn. Subtle signs are the feather-light nudges. The ones you can easily talk yourself out of. They can be a thought that pops into your mind "out of nowhere." A feeling of yes or no with no logical reason attached. Maybe a soft, energetic pull toward something such as a person, a place, a book, or an idea. A common one is seeing something once or twice that feels a little off, but familiar.

Subtle signs are your spirit guides trying to get your attention without interrupting your day. They feel natural, almost woven into your own thoughts. They don't demand, they invite. These are the signs people dismiss the most because they're quiet enough to blend into the noise, but subtle doesn't mean weak. Subtle signs are often your spirit guides at their wisest, when they are especially gentle, steady, and allowing you to choose.

Obvious signs are the ones that feel as if your spirit guides went from whispering to waving a flare. They are a symbol or number pattern repeating so often that it borders on comedy. A song showing up at exactly the right moment, often multiple times. A "coincidence" that is frankly too on-the-nose to be random. A message in a book, on a billboard, a license plate, or even a social media post delivered with perfect timing. You think of someone, and they immediately call or text. Something happens moments after you ask for guidance.

Obvious signs feel personal, targeted, and often a little ridiculous, but in the best way. These are the signs designed to stop you in your tracks and make you go, "Okay… that cannot be a coincidence."

The Many Ways Your Spirit Guides Send Signs

Once you start paying attention, it becomes obvious there are signs. Keep in mind, your spirit guides are creative. They don't limit themselves to one method. They use whatever is easiest for you to notice, whatever feels most natural to your personality, and whatever will attract your attention with the most meaning in the moment. Think of signs like a whole conversation happening across your day. Not one big message, but a series of winks, nudges, clues, and echoes designed to catch your attention long enough for you to notice that something feels different. Let's walk through the most common kinds.

1. Patterns that tap you on the shoulder. Numbers, symbols, or shapes that you'll often see in repetition. Maybe the clock reads 11:11 right as you think about your next big step. Maybe a certain number follows you everywhere for a week in the form of receipts, license plates, billboards, or timestamps. It's not about the number itself. It's the timing, the frequency, and the way it sparks your awareness. Repetition is one of the spirit guide's favorite highlighters. When you see them, pay attention. The moment matters.

2. Music with weirdly perfect timing. Your spirit guides absolutely use music like a universal playlist queued up only for you. A song comes on that matches your exact emotion, or answers a question you've been wrestling with, or reminds you of a loved one you need to feel closer to. No, it's not random that it happens twice in one day, and the lyrics hit you in the heart. Music bypasses logic and speaks straight to the intuitive part of you where your spirit guides hang out. They know that.

3. Animals that show up as messengers. Sometimes, it's a bird landing right in your path (that's a big one for me).

Sometimes, it's the same kind of animal popping up three times in twenty-four hours. Sometimes, it's an unusual behavior, such as a deer stopping to stare at you longer than a deer should reasonably be staring at a person. Animals are powerful carriers of meaning because they draw your focus in a heartbeat. Your spirit guides take full advantage of that. If an animal interaction feels loaded, that's your sign.

But here's the thing that people often confuse. An animal showing up as a sign does not automatically make it your spirit animal. Most of the time, it's simply a message using the quickest available symbol. That raccoon that crossed your path might be pointing you toward clarity, strength, or perspective, not applying for a permanent position in your spiritual entourage. Signs are usually situational, not identity-level. So when an animal shows up, you don't need to adopt it, claim it, or assign it a forever meaning. Ask yourself what the moment is trying to show you. Your spirit guides use the natural world because it's easy for you to notice, and because it speaks in symbolism you instinctively understand, even if you can't put it into words right away.

4. Words that feel aimed straight at you. You're scrolling and stop on one sentence. You overhear someone in line at the grocery store say exactly what you needed to hear. A quote in a book feels as if it was placed there by someone who knew what you were dealing with. Spirit guides will use any text or voice that's already in your environment. It's effortless for them.

5. Objects that seem random… until they aren't. They are a feather on your doorstep, a coin (especially dimes) in an odd place, or a crystal you forgot about falling off a shelf. It's an old photo turning up when you need a reminder of who you used to be. Physical signs are ground-

ing. They're the kind of communication you can literally hold in your hand or carry in your pocket.

6. Synchronicities that feel scripted. When you think of someone, and they text. You ask for guidance from your spirit guides and, boom, a solution appears. You're struggling with a decision, and all the pieces fall into place like a cosmic Tetris game snapping perfectly into alignment. Synchronicity is one of your spirit guides' clearest "pay attention" languages. It's not about coincidence. It's about flow and events lining up with such eerie precision that you'd be lying to yourself to call it accidental.

7. Physical sensations and energetic shifts. Not everything is visual or external. Sometimes, a sign shows up in your body. A chill down your spine at the exact right moment, or a warm pressure when you're being guided toward something. It could be a calming wave when you finally choose the option that aligns with your path. Your body is an antenna. Your spirit guides use it because it's direct and immediate, and you can't miss it when you drop into awareness.

8. Inner knowing. This is the sign that feels like it came from inside you and is the quietest and often the hardest to trust. It's the sense of knowing something without evidence. An idea that arrives complete, with no assembling required, or a decision that suddenly feels obvious even though nothing has changed. This is guidance coming through your intuition, your higher mind. It's not flashy, but it's reliable, and if you're honest, you've followed this before, even when you didn't have a name for it.

9. Dreams that carry messages. Some dreams are only brain clutter, but some have weight. They convey clarity or strong emotion and stay with you. They deliver insights you didn't have before you went to bed. Your spirit guides

use dreams because your resistance is offline, your doubt is sleeping, and the intuitive part of you is wide awake.

10. People showing up as messengers. A stranger says something that hits home, or a friend recommends exactly the right book. Someone shares a story that answers a question you hadn't voiced out loud. Spirit guides often use people because we're already listening to them. Sometimes, humans are walking, talking billboards for the spirit guides.

The magic isn't the category, it's the moment. Signs aren't here to impress you. They're here to guide you, and the more you start noticing them, the more you realize that your spirit guides have been speaking to you in a hundred tiny ways. You simply didn't know the conversation had already begun.

Spotting Your Personal Sign Language

Let's take a time out and help you build some awareness. Not by forcing signs to appear, but by noticing the ones already weaving through your day.

Step 1: Look Back Before You Look Forward

Think of the last week or two. Don't overthink it. Write down three moments that made you pause even a little bit. It could be anything. Maybe a number that kept popping up, or a random object you found, or a conversation you overheard. It could be an animal encounter that felt strangely significant. Don't judge them. Just capture them.

Step 2: Notice the Pattern

Look at your three moments and ask yourself what feeling came from them. Was it comfort? Curiosity? Reassurance? A sense of "that's weird"? Spirit guides speak through emotions as much as symbols. Circle the one that gave you the strongest internal "ping."

Step 3: Ask the Key Question

For the circled moment, finish this sentence: "This got my attention because…" Don't aim for perfection. Aim for honesty. Often the meaning reveals itself through the simplest observation.

What you did was train your awareness to recognize the difference between noise and nudges, and here's the beautiful truth. If you can spot three of these moments from your past week, you can absolutely spot them as they happen going forward. You're not creating anything out of thin air. You're simply tuning into what's been whispering to you all along. Trust what stood out, trust what you felt, and trust that this is the beginning of a much clearer conversation with your spirit guides.

When You Miss a Sign (Because Everyone Does)

Missing a sign doesn't frustrate your spirit guides. They're not tapping their feet as if they are impatient spiritual parents. They simply shift their strategy. If the whisper doesn't connect with you, they try something a little louder. If that doesn't work, they try something even clearer. It's all gentle, all supportive, and all designed to help you notice what's already trying to reach you.

One of the simplest ways they escalate is through repetition. A sign that appeared once now appears again… and again. It circles back into your awareness with the kind of persistence that makes you pause and think, "Didn't I just see this?" When the same number pattern, symbol, phrase, or feeling keeps looping into your day like a cosmic rerun, that's your spirit guides patiently raising their hand a little higher.

But repetition isn't the only tool they use. If one "channel" isn't getting your attention, spirit guides will switch the medium entirely. Maybe you didn't catch the numbers, so they try a song. Maybe you brushed off the song, so they nudge a dream. Maybe you ignored the intuitive pull, so they drop the message into a perfectly timed conversation with someone in your life. It's not a scavenger hunt. It's your spirit guides checking every door to see which one you're actually listening through.

And when a message is truly important, one of those "please don't miss this" moments, your spirit guides will sometimes let the external world rearrange itself around you. A plan falls apart, so you'll finally take another path, or a door closes so a better one can open. Maybe a coincidence becomes so uncanny it borders on comedic. These big shifts aren't punishment. They're protection. It's your spirit guides doing their thing even when you're too overwhelmed, distracted, or unsure to recognize the earlier nudges. The bottom line? Escalation is love in motion. Your spirit guides don't get louder because you're doing anything wrong. They get louder because they're invested in helping you stay aligned with what's right for you.

Your Turn: A Simple Sign-Spotting Practice

Your spirit guides have been waiting for this part. Before you move on to the next chapter, try this short assignment. It's easy, it's practical, and it works because it teaches your brain exactly what your intuition already knows.

First, choose a sign category. Pick one area where you want to become more aware. Not all, just one. For example, numbers and patterns, animal encounters, or words you overhear or read. Choose the one that feels like your natural doorway.

Next, set a forty-eight-hour awareness window. For the next two days, don't go hunting. Don't try to force anything. Simply make a quiet agreement with your spirit guides: "If you've been trying to reach me, I'm paying attention now." That's it. That's the whole contract.

Over the next two days, notice one thing that stands out. Your job isn't to interpret yet. Your job is to notice. Write down something that catches your attention, even if it seems tiny or silly or easy to dismiss. Ask yourself: what made it stand out? You might not know the exact meaning yet, but that's okay. You're training your awareness. You're practicing recognition, not analysis. Most importantly, you're letting your spirit guides meet you halfway. Remember, signs aren't a special event. They're already happening, and now you're learning how to see them.

6

Some Common Signs & Symbols

Spirit guides speak in hundreds of quiet ways, and they love using the everyday world as their canvas. A feather on your path, a flash of lightning, the sound of a bell… none of these moments are random when they come to you with meaning. They're part of a symbolic language that's been woven into human experience for centuries, a language your spirit guides use because it's simple, recognizable, and deeply personal.

You don't have to memorize every possible sign or decode them the way you'd study for an exam. These messages work because of how they feel when they arrive. They catch your attention, tug at your intuition, and make you pause long enough to sense the truth underneath. Your spirit guides meet you where you are, using symbols you're likely to notice, understand, and connect with in your own way.

Although there are many books on this topic, I wanted to provide this short list of common signs I am most familiar with (and see a lot of!) that your spirit guides love to use. Each one carries its own flavor of guidance, comfort, or clarity. As you move through them, keep your heart open, your curiosity awake, and your intuition engaged. You'll soon discover that the world around you is far more alive, responsive, and intentional than it ever seemed before.

Keeping a Signs & Symbols Log

Before you dive into the list, I want to offer you a simple way to make these signs feel more personal and meaningful over time. Consider keeping a short signs and symbols log. This doesn't need to be fancy or time-consuming. It can be a notebook, a notes app on your phone, or even a running list in a journal. When something catches your attention, whether it is a feather, a coin, an animal encounter, a repeating symbol, or a moment that makes you pause, write down what you noticed, where you were, and what you were thinking or feeling at the time. That's it. You don't need to interpret it right away or assign it a meaning. This is about noticing, not decoding.

Over time, patterns will start to emerge. You'll see which symbols show up for you most often and how they tend to align with what's happening in your life. This log becomes your personal sign language, a record of how your spirit guides communicate with you. The more you acknowledge what you notice, the clearer the conversation becomes.

Hawk

We are helping you see the bigger picture.

When a hawk appears, your spirit guides are inviting you to rise above the noise and look at your life from a higher, clearer vantage point. Hawks don't waste energy on distractions. They soar until the path reveals itself. Their presence signals that clarity is available to you now, not through frantic searching, but through stepping back and seeing the situation as a whole. If a hawk catches your attention, pause and take note of what's happening in your life, rethink your priorities, or trust the intuitive insight that's been circling in your mind.

Feather

We are watching over you.

When you see a feather, your spirit guides are offering a gentle reminder that you are protected, loved, and supported. Feathers often appear during times when you need reassurance or a quiet confirmation that you're not walking this path alone. Their softness and lightness symbolize ease, trust, and the subtle ways guidance can drift into your life when you're open to it. If a feather catches your attention, pause and receive its message. Your spirit guides are reaching out with comfort, wrapping you in their presence, and reminding you that you are watched over every step of the way.

Coin

We are sending resources.

When a coin appears unexpectedly, your spirit guides are offering a clear reminder that you are supported in both practical and meaningful ways. Coins often show up during times when you're thinking about resources, stability, or your next steps, bringing quiet confirmation that help is available. Their weight and shine symbolize opportunity, aligned timing, and the tangible ways guidance can show up in your physical world. If a coin finds you, pause and acknowledge it as a message of abundance. Your spirit guides are opening doors, smoothing your path, and reminding you that you don't have to figure everything out alone.

Bell Sound

We are trying to get your attention.

When you hear a bell sound, your spirit guides are offering a clear invitation to pause and pay attention. Bells often ring, whether physically, subtly, or in your mind, during moments when guidance is trying to reach you, signaling that something important is unfolding. Their bright tone symbolizes clarity, awakening, and the way truth can cut through distraction when you're open to hearing it. If a bell catches your awareness, take a breath and tune in. Your spirit guides are calling you into the present moment, helping you notice what you might otherwise overlook, and guiding you toward the insight they want you to receive.

Butterfly

We are helping you transform.

When you see a butterfly, your spirit guides are reminding you that transformation is taking place, even if it feels subtle or slow. Butterflies often appear during periods of inner growth, healing, or change, offering reassurance that you're stepping into a new version of yourself. Their delicate wings symbolize lightness, freedom, and the beauty that comes from releasing old patterns and trusting the process. If a butterfly catches your attention, take a moment to acknowledge the shift happening within you. Your spirit guides are gently affirming that you're emerging, evolving, and ready for what comes next.

Heart Shape

We are sending you love.

When you see a heart or heart shape appear unexpectedly, whether in a rock, a leaf, a cloud, or a shadow, your spirit guides are sending a gentle reminder that you are loved, supported, and held. These natural heart signs often show up when you need emotional reassurance or a moment of connection, quietly affirming that you're not alone. Their familiar shape symbolizes compassion, comfort, and the invisible threads of love that tie you to your spirit guides and the universe itself. If a heart shape catches your attention, pause and receive it. Your spirit guides are reaching out with tenderness, wrapping you in emotional support and reminding you that love surrounds you in every step you take.

Hummingbirds

We are bringing joy to your path.

When you see a hummingbird, your spirit guides are bringing joy and lightness into your path. These tiny messengers often appear during times when your energy needs lifting or when a moment of beauty can shift your perspective. Their quick, shimmering movements symbolize vibrancy, resilience, and the ability to find sweetness even in challenging moments. If a hummingbird catches your attention, pause and take in the moment. Your spirit guides are inviting you to embrace joy in the present, reminding you that even small bursts of wonder can bring the clarity and encouragement your heart needs.

Lightning

We are illuminating your way.

When you see lightning, your spirit guides are igniting clarity and sudden insight. Lightning often appears during moments when a shift is needed or when truth is ready to break through old patterns. Its quick, powerful flash symbolizes illumination, awakening, and the kind of understanding that comes all at once rather than slowly over time. If lightning captures your attention, pause and feel what's rising within you. Your spirit guides are high-lighting a moment of realization, urging you to notice what has become clear and to trust the breakthrough that's unfolding.

Flickering Light

We are gently guiding your awareness.

When you notice a flickering light, your spirit guides are signaling subtle shifts around you. This gentle change in illumination often appears during moments when energy is moving, when your intuition is awakening, or when your guides want to remind you of their presence in a quiet, unobtrusive way. The soft pulse of a light symbol-izes transition, awareness, and the delicate ways guidance can make itself known without overwhelming your senses. If a flickering light draws your attention, pause and tune in. Your spirit guides are encouraging you to notice the energies at play, trust what you feel, and stay open to the messages unfolding around you.

Key

We are opening the way for you.

When you see a key, your spirit guides are opening a new path or opportunity. Keys often appear when something is ready to unlock in your life, like clarity, access, direction, or a shift you've been preparing for. Their shape symbolizes answers, entry points, and the movement from confusion into understanding. If a key catches your attention, pause and reflect on what might be ready to open. Your spirit guides are showing you that you have access to the next step, encouraging you to trust the doorway that's revealing itself and walk through with confidence.

Rainbow

We are reminding you that hope still exists.

When you see a rainbow, your spirit guides are offering reassurance during or after a challenging moment. Rainbows often appear when emotions have been stirred, when clarity is returning, or when you're coming out of a period of uncertainty. Their arc across the sky symbolizes promise, balance, and the idea that contrast is part of growth. If a rainbow catches your attention, pause and let it sink in. Your spirit guides are reminding you that storms don't last forever, that beauty can follow difficulty, and that something lighter is possible even if you can't see the full picture yet.

Dragonfly

We are asking you to see beneath the surface.

When a dragonfly appears, your spirit guides are inviting you to look beyond appearances and trust deeper truths. Dragonflies often show up when perception is shifting or when you're being nudged to question assumptions you've been holding onto. Their iridescent wings symbolize insight, adaptability, and the ability to move between emotional and intuitive layers with ease. If a dragonfly draws your attention, pause and reflect on what might not be as it seems. Your spirit guides are encouraging you to lean into wisdom, clarity, and the perspective that comes from inner awareness rather than surface-level understanding.

Song Lyrics

We are speaking to you directly.

When specific song lyrics stand out or seem to repeat at exactly the right moment, your spirit guides are using sound to reach you. Music has a way of slipping past logic and going straight to the heart, making it a powerful channel for guidance. Lyrics often appear when you're seeking confirmation, comfort, or encouragement, mirroring exactly what you're thinking or feeling. If a song line grabs your attention, pause and listen closely. Your spirit guides are communicating through familiarity and emotion, offering insight in a way that feels personal, timely, and unmistakably meant for you.

Sudden Familiar Scent

We are close to you right now.

When you notice a sudden scent with no clear source, such as flowers, perfume, smoke, or something comforting, your spirit guides are signaling their presence. These moments often happen during reflection, emotional processing, or when you need grounding and reassurance.

Scents are deeply tied to memory and emotion, symbolizing connection, comfort, and the unseen bonds that surround you. If a scent catches your awareness, pause and breathe it in. Your spirit guides are reminding you that you are supported in ways that go beyond what you can see, offering quiet companionship and reassurance.

Animal Crossing Your Path

We are guiding your timing.

When an animal crosses your path unexpectedly, whether it's a deer, cat, bird, or another creature that makes you pause, your spirit guides are drawing attention to timing and direction. These moments often occur when you're rushing, distracted, or questioning your next move. The interruption itself is part of the message. Animals symbolize instinct, presence, and alignment with natural flow. If an animal crossing stops you in your tracks, take a breath. Your spirit guides are encouraging you to slow down, stay alert, and trust that even small pauses can realign you with where you're meant to go.

As you begin noticing these signs more often, trust what speaks to you and let the rest simply exist as part of the world's beauty. Your relationship with your spirit guides is personal, evolving, and uniquely yours, and these symbols are only one of the many ways they reach out. Over time, you'll develop your own list and shorthand with them. You'll have your own vocabulary of feathers, bells, butterflies, and moments of sudden clarity. Let it unfold naturally. Pay attention to what lights up inside you. And remember, your spirit guides are always finding ways to connect with you. Sometimes softly, sometimes boldly, but always with love.

7

When Numbers Nudge You

If you've ever glanced at the clock at exactly the same time day after day or noticed a string of repeating numbers on receipts, license plates, or street addresses, you're already familiar with one of the most common ways spirit guides send messages. Numbers catch our attention in a way few other signs do. They're quick, they're precise, and they can slip into your day without interrupting anything.

Repeating numbers aren't spooky or complicated. They're simply a universal language your spirit guides use to tap you on the shoulder. The patterns themselves carry meaning, but just as important is the moment they appear in relation to what you were thinking, feeling, questioning, or worrying about. Numbers show up as reassurance, redirection, or confirmation, often exactly when you need a little clarity or encouragement.

Before we dive into the individual number meanings, it helps to know how to read them in practice. These numbers aren't meant to be treated like rigid rules or fortune-cookie predictions. Think of them as themes your spirit guides use to highlight what's already unfolding in your life. The meaning doesn't live in the number alone. It lives in the moment you notice it. The definitions that follow are meant to give you a shared language with your spirit guides, not a checklist to memorize. As you read through them, pay attention to which ones feel familiar, comforting, or oddly personal. Those are usually the numbers already working with you.

111 — Alignment, Intuition, and Your Inner Green Light

If there were a celebrity number in the spiritual world, 111 (and its flashier sibling, 1111) would win the crown. These numbers show up when your energy, intention, and inner guidance are aligning in a meaningful way. It's the cosmic equivalent of catching every green light on your drive. When you see 111, your spirit guides are calling your attention to what you're thinking or feeling in that exact moment. It often appears when your thoughts are beginning to manifest more quickly, or when you're edging closer to something important such as inspiration, insight, a decision, or a new beginning

When 1111 appears, it's the same message but with fireworks. It's a heightened nudge to pay attention because something significant is aligning in your inner or outer world. Many people experience 1111 as an "awakening number" or a sign that your intuitive senses are opening and the connection with your spirit guides is strengthening. It often marks a shift in awareness, a moment when you're stepping more fully onto your real path, even if you don't realize it yet. Whether it's 111 or 1111, the message is clear. You're aligned, you're supported and you're being invited to lean into your intuition.

222 — Balance, Patience, and Trust

When 222 shows up, your spirit guides are reminding you that things are coming together even if you can't see the full picture yet. It's a gentle nudge to stay steady and trust the timing. This number often appears when you're waiting on something, second-guessing yourself, or needing reassurance that you haven't taken a wrong turn.

333 — Support, Encouragement, and Guidance

Seeing 333 is like getting a spiritual group hug. It's a sign that your spirit guides are close, paying attention, and actively supporting you. This number tends to show up when you're working hard, navigating growth, or pushing through doubt.

444 — Protection and Stability

444 is the classic "you are safe" number. When it appears, your spirit guides are offering energetic protection and grounding. It often shows up during stressful times or when you're taking on something new and slightly scary. The message isn't to stop, it's to know you're supported as you move forward.

555 — Change, Shifts, and Transformation

When 555 pops into your world, something is gearing up to change. Sometimes it's an internal shift, like a new perspective, a new idea, or a new clarity. Other times, it's something in your outer world beginning to rearrange. Either way, it's a sign to stay adaptable and open. Your spirit guides aren't warning you. They're preparing you for movement.

666 — Realignment, Grounding, and Recalibration

Despite its reputation, 666 in spiritual communication is not negative. It appears when your mind is racing, your energy is scattered, or you're focusing too much on worry or fear. This number brings you back to center. It encourages you to breathe, simplify, and return to what matters.

777 — Spiritual Insight and Deeper Inner Wisdom

When 777 appears, your spirit guides are encouraging you to look within. It's a sign that your intuition is speaking more clearly and that you may be ready for a new level of understanding or spiritual growth. This number often shows up during reflective times, healing work, or big moments of clarity.

888 — Abundance, Momentum, and Flow

888 is all about expansion, including energetic, emotional, financial, or creative development (or growth). When you see it, your spirit guides are showing you that something is opening. Opportunities, movement, or progress is underway. It's a confirmation number, signaling that you're stepping into a more aligned and abundant phase.

999 — Completion, Closure, and Release

999 appears when something is wrapping up, whether

it's a chapter, a habit, a belief, or a situation you've outgrown. Your spirit guides aren't pushing you out the door. They're showing you what's naturally ending so you can make space for what's next. Closure isn't always dramatic. Sometimes it's simply a shift.

Repeating numbers are one of the simplest, most accessible ways your spirit guides get your attention. They slip into your day without fanfare, but when you pause long enough to notice them, they can deliver incredible clarity. You don't have to memorize every meaning or decode them like a secret language. What matters most is how you feel in the moment they appear, what you were thinking about, and what part of your life the message seems to touch. Consider these numbers little breadcrumbs on your spiritual path. They are small reminders that you're guided, supported, and part of something larger than whatever is happening in front of you. You're not imagining the timing. You're not "looking for signs." You're learning to recognize the ones already there.

As you begin noticing repeating numbers more often, don't overthink them. Smile at them. Acknowledge them. Let them be tiny winks from your spirit guides reminding you that you're aligned, you're growing, and you're connected. Your spirit guides love finding ways to reach you, and numbers happen to be one of their favorites. Now that you know how to interpret them, you'll never see 1111 the same way again.

Ironically, as you start noticing signs and repeating numbers more often, it's completely natural for doubt to creep in. You might wonder if you're reading too much into things, imagining patterns, or just noticing what you want to see. That questioning doesn't mean you're doing this wrong. It means you're becoming aware. Doubt is often the very next layer that surfaces once intuition wakes up, like fog rolling in after the sun rises. In the next chapter, we're going to talk about that fog, including where it comes from, why it's so common, and how to gently clear it without shutting yourself down or second-guessing every sign you receive. Because learning to trust guidance isn't about never doubting. It's about knowing what to do when doubt shows up.

8

Clearing the Doubt Fog

Doubt isn't a sign you're doing anything wrong. It's a sign you're alive, thinking, and trying. If you've ever questioned whether your intuition is real, whether your spirit guides are actually nudging you, or whether you're making it all up… congratulations. You're officially human.

Self-doubt shows up whenever we reach for something bigger than our comfort zone. It's the brain's job to keep us safe, and "safe" often means "familiar." So when you start exploring your spiritual senses, your intuition, your connection to your spirit guides, and the quiet knowing beneath the noise, your mind does what minds do: it raises an eyebrow and whispers, "Are you sure about this?" That whisper isn't proof that your spiritual path is off-track. It's proof you're opening.

Even the most intuitive people I know experience doubt. In fact, the deeper your trust becomes, the more likely old patterns of uncertainty will try one last encore. Doubt isn't the enemy of spiritual connection. It's a companion on the journey. It keeps you discerning. It keeps you grounded. But if you let it take the wheel? Suddenly your spirit guides have to wave road flares to get your attention. The real work isn't eliminating doubt. It's learning how to recognize its voice, soothe it, and keep walking anyway.

My Relationship with Doubt

I'll be the first to admit I experience doubt constantly. I doubt my intuition, my connections, my decisions, and, ironically, my ability to write a book on spirit guides while wrestling with my own questions about them. But here's the truth. The doubt never actually stopped me. It tried. Oh, it tried. But every time I felt that familiar swirl of *Who am I to write this?* I took a breath, listened deeper, and kept typing. Not because I had perfect clarity, but because I wanted to show up anyway. This book isn't being written from a mountaintop of certainty. It's being written from the real, messy middle where doubt and faith coexist. If I can keep moving through it, you can too.

It surprises a lot of people but doubt often gets louder when your connection to your spirit guides is getting stronger, not weaker. Think of it like stepping into brighter light, and suddenly you notice every speck of dust floating around. As your intuition sharpens and the signs get clearer, your old belief systems don't pack their bags and leave. They push back. They test the new foundation you're building. Your mind is trying to reconcile your expanding spiritual experiences with years (or decades) of being told to be logical, practical, or skeptical. So when your spirit guides start nudging you more often, or the signs become impossible to ignore, the part of you that's used to being in control shows up with a clipboard and demands to know what is happening.

That internal friction doesn't mean you're "off track."

It means you're stretching into something bigger than what you previously believed was possible. Doubt shows up because your old self is trying to understand your new growth. It's a sign you're getting closer to your spirit guides, to your intuition, and to the version of you who trusts her own inner compass.

Where All That Doubt Comes From

A big source of doubt is simple social conditioning. Most of us grew up in a world that treats anything metaphysical as suspicious at best and imaginary at worst. We're encouraged to trust spreadsheets, calendars, and "cold hard facts," but not the subtle knowing in our chest or the flicker of guidance that comes out of nowhere. So, of course, metaphysics can feel "unreal."

We weren't taught to work with intuition the way we were taught to work with email. Nobody sat us down in school and said, "Here's how to recognize a nudge from your spirit guides." Instead, we learned to dismiss anything that couldn't be measured, graded, or explained in a PowerPoint. All that conditioning doesn't disappear overnight. It lingers, it whispers, and when you start stepping into your spiritual life, those old messages get triggered. The key is realizing they're not truth… they're training you've outgrown.

Then there is fear, logic, and upbringing. They are a trio that can shut down spiritual connection faster than a flicked light switch. Fear tells you you're imagining things. Logic says, "Be serious, that's not how the world works." And upbringing, well, that one can be the loudest of all. Many of us were raised to believe intuition was unreliable, spirituality was "out there," or that anything you couldn't touch was nonsense. Put those three together and no wonder you sometimes feel a little crazy when you sense a message, a nudge, or a presence that doesn't fit the old rules. But none of these things mean you're wrong. They simply mean you're human. You were trained to navigate life from the neck up, and now you're learning to live from the soul out. That transition can be disorienting, but it's also where the magic begins.

How Your Spirit Guides See Your Doubt (Spoiler: with Zero Judgment)

The beautiful thing, maybe the most comforting thing, is how your spirit guides see your doubt. They don't roll their eyes or get impatient. They don't judge you for hesitating or second-guessing. To them, your doubt is part of the human experience. They understand that living in a physical body with a busy mind is noisy, confusing, and overwhelming sometimes. So when you question yourself, your spirit guides don't pull away, they lean in. They soften. They adjust. They find gentler ways to reach you. They're not grading your spiritual performance. They're walking alongside you with absolute compassion, knowing every moment of uncertainty is simply another step toward trust. To them, your doubt isn't a failure, it's a sign you're trying, learning, and opening, and they love you for that.

Spotting Your Doubts (and Softening Their Grip)

Grab your journal or notebook or whatever you're using and try this:

1. Identify a doubt. Think of one place where doubt shows up the most. Maybe it's trusting a sign, believing a

nudge, or wondering if you're truly connected. Pick just one. Keeping it simple helps the clarity rise. Write it down.

2. Ask where it comes from. Now, look at that doubt like you would examine a pebble in your hand. Ask yourself some questions: Whose voice is this? Is it fear trying to keep me safe? Is it a leftover belief from my upbringing? Or is it perfectionism trying to avoid mistakes? Naming the source often reveals that the doubt isn't you. It's old programming.

3. Choose one tiny next step. Not a giant leap. A pebble-sized movement forward. Write a paragraph about how you want to react to the doubt you wrote down. Will you trust the sign you got yesterday rather than discount it? Ask for another nudge? Say yes to the thing that's been circling you? Your spirit guides never expect perfection. They only need you to be willing to take one small step through the fog.

4. Notice how the doubt shifts. It may soften, it may shrink, or it may simply sit quietly instead of shouting. But each time you move through doubt instead of surrendering to it, you're teaching your mind a new pattern that you are allowed to trust yourself.

How Doubting Your Spirit Guides Derails Your Manifesting

When it comes to manifesting, your spirit guides are your biggest teammates, quietly steering opportunities your way, nudging you toward aligned choices, and helping you hold the vision when your mind wants to spiral. But if you constantly doubt their presence or second-guess every sign, you are blocking the very support you've been asking for.

Manifesting requires clarity, and doubt scatters that

clarity like confetti in a windstorm. One part of you is trying to call in what you want, while another part is questioning whether the guidance helping you get there is even real. That inner split makes it harder for your spirit guides to line things up for you. Not because they're offended, but because you're unintentionally dismissing the "GPS signals" they keep trying to send. The more you trust their involvement, even in small ways, the smoother and more aligned your manifestations become.

Building Trust One Small Step at a Time

Trust doesn't usually arrive in a lightning bolt. It doesn't sweep in with trumpets, a choir, and a neon sign that says, "YES, THIS IS REAL." For most of us, trust shows up in tiny moments. As small, almost forgettable shifts that slowly add up until one day you realize you're not doubting every little thing anymore.

Think of trust as strengthening a new muscle. You don't go to the gym once and walk out ready to lift a car. You build strength by showing up, trying, wobbling a little, and then trying again. Trust in your spirit guides works exactly the same way. It grows each time you follow a small nudge, and it turns out well. It expands every time you listen to your intuition instead of your fear. It deepens when you notice a sign and decide, just this once, to believe it's meant for you.

Here's the best part. Your spirit guides don't need you to make giant leaps. They're not asking for blind faith or spiritual perfection. They're thrilled with baby steps, micro-acts of trust, and little moments where you think that maybe this is real. When you take those small steps, something beautiful happens. Your spirit guides respond.

They match your movement with their own. They make the next sign a little clearer, the next nudge a little stronger, and the path a little smoother. Before you know it, you look back and realize you've strung together an entire trail of tiny brave choices that led you somewhere you didn't believe you could go. This is how trust is built. Not all at once, but moment by moment, step by step, heart open enough to let a little more in each time.

What Happens When You Start Trusting (Even a Little)

Once you start taking those small steps toward trust, the entire relationship with your spirit guides begins to shift. Not because they change, but because you do. You start noticing things you used to overlook. A thought that comes out of nowhere has a different texture to it. A sign you would have brushed off two months ago hits you with a quiet, steady *yes*. You begin to feel accompanied rather than alone. Slowly, almost imperceptibly at first, your inner landscape reorganizes itself around connection rather than skepticism.

The more you trust, the more guidance flows. Not because you've "earned" it, but because you've lowered the internal static enough to hear it. Your intuition sharpens, synchronicities multiply, manifestation becomes easier, and your life takes on a sense of support, timing, and gentle orchestration that you may never have noticed before. Trust doesn't make life perfect, but it does allow everything to be real, and once you've felt that, even for a blink, you'll never unknow it.

A Moment for Honest Reflection

Set aside a few minutes, grab your journal, and take yourself through these questions with kindness and zero judgment.

1. When was the last time I trusted a small nudge and it worked out? Big or tiny, look for any moment where following a "feeling" led you somewhere good. Let yourself acknowledge it.

2. What would one baby step toward trust look like for me this week? Something small such as asking for a sign, listening instead of dismissing, following one intuitive pull, or simply saying "Maybe this is real."

3. And finally… what do I want my relationship with doubt to be moving forward? You don't have to banish it. You simply have to decide its role. Background noise? A gentle signal? A companion you can nod at and walk past? Write whatever comes. There is no wrong answer, only honesty, openness, and the next step on your path.

As you move into the next part of your journey, keep this close: doubt doesn't disqualify you from connection. It doesn't make you less intuitive, less spiritual, or less capable. It certainly doesn't make you any less worthy of guidance. Your spirit guides aren't waiting for you to become fearless or flawless. They're simply waiting for you to stay open. One breath, one nudge, and one small act of trust at a time. Remember that you don't have to silence every doubt to walk this path. You just have to decide that doubt won't be the thing that stops you.

As the doubt begins to thin and your trust settles in, something subtle but important shifts. The signs stop feeling random. The nudges feel a little more intentional. And you may start to sense that there's more than only guidance happening, there's presence. Up to now, you've been learning how to notice, interpret, and trust communication. Next, we're going to move closer to the source itself. Because once the fog clears, it becomes easier to recognize who's been walking with you all along. In the next chapter, we'll talk about meeting your spirit guide team, not in a dramatic, movie-scene way, but in the grounded, personal way that connection usually unfolds.

9

Meet Your Spirit Guide Team

You don't have to trek through a forest at midnight, chant in ancient languages, or wait for lightning to strike in the shape of your initials to meet your spirit guides. The truth is simpler, softer, and way more personal: your team already knows you. They know your quirks, your dreams, your stubborn streak, your sense of humor, and every version of you that you've ever been. It's finally time to meet them back.

Don't think of it as summoning. It's remembering. It's reconnecting with the energetic support system that's been with you from your very first inhale. Most people never learn who's on their team because they expect a parade float announcement, but spirit guides show up in subtler ways with nudges, synchronicities, emotions, knowing, and tiny flashes of insight.

How to Sense Who's on Your Team

The easiest place to start is with the energy you feel. Every spirit guide has a distinct "signature" like their energetic fingerprint, and your body is already wired to pick up on it. You don't need psychic training. You simply need to pay attention. Here are the simplest ways to start recognizing who's with you:

1. Notice the emotional shift. Spirit guides often reveal themselves through how they feel, not how they look. One guide might bring calm confidence. Another might feel similar to a quiet warmth. Another might bring clarity or sudden focus. You've felt these shifts before. You just didn't label them as your spirit guide stepping in. Ask yourself: "What emotion shows up when I settle into stillness?" That emotion is usually tied to a specific spirit guide.

2. Pay attention to your body's reactions. Your physical body responds to your spirit guides the way it responds to people in a room. It is subtle (usually), instinctive, and automatic. You may feel things like a tingling at the crown of your head, a warmth in your chest, a cool breeze on your cheek, or even a gentle buzz in your hands. Each spirit guide tends to have a consistent "calling card." Once you notice it a few times, you'll start recognizing who's stepping forward.

3. Track where your thoughts suddenly shift. Something such as a new idea drops in without any buildup. Maybe it's a sudden solution, a calm truth, a direction, or a reminder. Those signal you're not alone in the room. Spirit guides communicate through thought all the time. A certain spirit guide may speak in logic and structure. Another may nudge you emotionally. Another might use humor or warmth. If the thought feels wiser than your current mood, that's a clue.

4. Look for patterns in your signs. Certain signs tend to repeat from the same spirit guide. Coins, feathers, numbers, animals, dreams, songs, or overheard words can all signal that a spirit guide is near. When a pattern shows

up three times or more, that's not random. That's a spirit guide trying to introduce itself.

How to Identify the Different Types of Spirit Guides You Might Have

Most people have more than one spirit guide (I'm pretty sure I have at least three regular players, but I'm still learning, exactly like you), but they don't all feel the same. Your team is made up of different energies, each with its own role, and the easiest way to figure out who's who is simply noticing how they show up in your life. It's okay if you don't feel all these different spirit guides. These are simply the most common. Yours will always be unique to you.

You'll likely sense one spirit guide more strongly than the others. It's a steady, familiar presence that seems to be there no matter what you're dealing with. This is often your primary spirit guide. Their energy tends to feel grounding, reliable, and unmistakably "yours," even if you can't explain why.

You may also notice a softer, more emotional presence. This is the spirit guide who steps in when your heart needs support. You will feel them during relationships, boundary issues, self-worth challenges, or moments when compassion is the lesson of the day. Their energy often feels warm and reassuring, similar to someone gently reminding you to breathe.

At certain times, you'll feel something very different. It will be a sharper, more alert sensation that nudges you toward safety or away from situations that aren't right. That's the protection spirit guide. They communicate through instincts, sudden clarity, or that full-body "nope" that appears before your mind even catches up.

Creative and insight-based spirit guides are a whole other flavor. They're the ones behind your ideas, your solutions, and your moments of brilliance while you're in the shower. Their energy feels quick, bright, and sometimes a little mischievous, like someone dropping hints and winking at you from behind the scenes.

Then there are the healing spirit guides, who show up in the quiet spaces. Their presence is gentler than the rest, often feeling cool, soothing, or subtle. They tend to appear when you're releasing old patterns, recovering emotionally, or finally ready to let go of something heavy. Their work is quiet but powerful.

You might also feel a spirit guide with a familiar edge, one that feels strangely personal or connected to your roots. That's usually an ancestor spirit guide. Not every ancestor becomes a spirit guide, but the ones who do often step forward with a feeling of recognition, as if you've known them forever without ever meeting.

And occasionally, you'll sense a broader, more expansive energy, the kind that delivers wisdom that feels bigger than you. These are the teaching spirit guides. They're the ones who push your growth, challenge your avoidance habits (yes, those), and hand you the uncomfortable truth wrapped in a bow.

Once you understand the energetic differences, it becomes much easier to tell which spirit guide is stepping forward. You're not trying to memorize categories. You're simply learning the personalities already woven into your inner world.

How to Start Building a Relationship with Each Spirit Guide

Getting to know your spirit guides isn't a one-time

introduction. It's a relationship, and the same as any relationship, it grows through simple, consistent moments of connection. You don't have to see them, hear them, or know their full résumé. You just need to start interacting with them in small, doable ways. Begin with the spirit guide you sense most easily. Pick the one whose energy feels familiar, steady, or simply present whenever you settle yourself. You don't need their name. Think of them the way you think of someone whose voice you recognize in a crowd, even if you can't see their face. Then, simply say hello (yes, I know that sounds a little bananas, but trust me on this. It works). It doesn't have to be in a ceremonial way.

Some spirit guides will respond through calmness. Some through ideas. Some through signs. Some through a sudden "you've got this" that wasn't there a moment ago. Pay attention to what shifts. That's how a relationship forms. Once you've said hello to one spirit guide, gently invite another to make themselves known. Their energy will feel different. Maybe lighter, maybe firmer, maybe more emotional or more expansive. Whatever shows up, treat it like meeting someone new at a comfortable coffee shop. No pressure, no expectations, only curiosity.

Then, acknowledge them when something clicks. Even a tiny "thank you for coming forward" strengthens the channel. Spirit guides don't need praise. They respond to awareness. Once you notice them, you feel them more clearly the next time. You're not trying to collect profiles. You're building trust one spirit guide at a time, one moment at a time, the same way you would with anyone who's helping you behind the scenes.

Let's Give This a Try

Find a quiet moment, nothing dramatic, just a few

minutes where you won't be interrupted. Sit comfortably, relax your body, and take one slow breath to settle yourself. Now, in your mind or out loud, say a simple "Hello." That's it. No chanting. No ritual. Simply a greeting.

Notice what happens next. Don't go hunting for something big. Instead, pay attention to the tiny things. Is there a shift in the air, a subtle emotional change, a warm feeling in your chest, a thought that comes out of nowhere, or even a calm sense of being met? Stay with whatever shows up for a moment. Let it be small. Let it be quiet. Your spirit guides are subtle because subtlety is how intuition speaks.

Then, take a moment to write down what you noticed. Even if it feels vague, even if you're not sure, especially if you're not sure, simply let the words flow without censoring them. Clarity builds through noticing, not perfection. If you'd like, repeat the same "hello" exercise tomorrow. And the next day. Over time, you'll start to recognize patterns. The spirit guide who feels steady, the one who feels warm, the one who drops ideas, and the one who protects. This is how relationships begin. One small moment, one quiet hello, and one honest observation at a time.

What to Do If You Don't Feel Anything Yet

If your "hello" felt like talking into an empty room, don't panic. This happens to more people than you think, and it has nothing to do with your worthiness, intuition level, or spiritual talent. It usually means you're trying too hard, thinking too much, or expecting fireworks when your spirit guides speak in whispers. Here's the truth. Some people sense their spirit guides immediately. Some need repetition and familiarity before anything registers. Neither path is wrong.

If you didn't feel anything, start smaller. Instead of

waiting for a sensation, look for a shift. Maybe a tiny pause between your thoughts, a calmer breath, or a slight emotional softening. Those subtle changes often are your spirit guides. You simply haven't learned to recognize their presence yet.

You can also change the approach. Try reaching out during a moment that already feels peaceful, such as right after waking up, during a walk, after journaling, or while drinking your morning coffee. Intuition is stronger when your mind isn't doing cartwheels. Don't underestimate consistency. A single "hello" is an introduction. A week of them becomes a conversation. Your spirit guides know you're trying, and they respond to effort far more easily than to perfection.

Finally, be honest with yourself. Sometimes "nothing" is actually fear, doubt, or old beliefs blocking your ability to notice what's already there. That's normal. You're opening a door you've never opened before, and the hinges might creak a little. Keep going anyway. You're not being ignored. You're learning a new language, and every attempt is progress, even when it feels empty.

A Personal Example

I've felt something around me my whole life. That quiet sense of not being entirely on my own, even when no one else was in the room. I didn't have language for it. I certainly didn't know you could introduce yourself to a spirit guide. That idea felt way too bold.

The first time I actually said "hello," it felt ridiculous. I was basically greeting thin air like an overly polite ghost host. Part of me was curious, but part of me was convinced I was talking to myself and should probably keep it down in case the neighbors heard me. But something interesting happened over time. The more I pushed past the awkwardness, the more I started noticing tiny changes, an emotional shift, a warm buzz in my chest, a sudden flash of clarity, or a feeling that someone had subtly stepped a little closer. It wasn't dramatic. It wasn't a movie moment. It was gentle, almost shy, but undeniably there.

The more I acknowledged those tiny responses, the easier it became to connect. What started as a hesitant "Um… hello?" turned into real conversations. Not out loud necessarily, but in the way I'd reach for guidance, get a nudge back, and realize I wasn't imagining it. It became a daily relationship. Something steady, comforting, and honestly kind of fun. These days, I communicate with my spirit guides every day, and the difference between then and now is simple: I stopped waiting for proof and started letting the relationship grow. If I can go from feeling silly to feeling supported, you absolutely can, too.

A Final Word

Getting to know your spirit guide team isn't about seeing visions or hearing voices. It's about learning to recognize support that's already woven into your life. Some days you'll feel it clearly. Some days you won't feel anything at all. Both are perfectly normal. What matters is that you're showing up. You're opening the door. You're practicing trust one small moment at a time.

Your spirit guides don't expect you to be perfect, psychic, or endlessly confident. They're not grading your progress. They simply want connections. They want those tiny invitations, quiet acknowledgments, and the willingness to believe that you're not navigating everything alone. Every time you reach out, even with the smallest "hello," you're building something real. You're strengthening a relationship that's been waiting patiently in the background of your life.

Keep going. Keep noticing. Keep trusting those first tiny nudges. You're doing better than you think, and your team is right there, cheering you on, even on the days when you can't feel them at all.

Now that you've begun to recognize your spirit guide team as something personal and real and not abstract or distant, the next step feels almost inevitable. Connection naturally invites conversation. In the next chapter, we're going to talk about how to communicate with your spirit guides in a way that feels natural, grounded, and pressure-free. No special language. No perfect technique. Just real, everyday ways to start talking to the team that's been listening all along.

10

Talking to Your Spirit Guides (Without Feeling Ridiculous)

There's a moment every spiritual seeker eventually faces that can't be avoided. It is that awkward pause where you open your mouth to talk to your spirit guides… and your brain immediately chimes in with, "Wow. We're really doing this. We're talking to thin air now?"

If this is you, welcome to the club. We all start here. There's no velvet rope or secret initiation. The door to communicating with your spirit guides opens the second you decide to knock.

Talking to your spirit guides isn't about "performing" spirituality. You don't need flowing robes or special imported incense. You don't have to get the words right. You don't even have to talk out loud if that feels too weird. Your spirit guides are tuned into you, the real you, in all your messy, grounded, human glory. If your voice cracks, they don't care. If you stumble, they're thrilled you're trying. If you feel silly at first, that actually means you're doing it right. You're stretching into a new way of relating to the unseen, and your ego isn't sure what to do with that.

Here's the part people forget: Talking to your spirit

guides is less about speaking and more about listening. They don't use English, Spanish, or the high school French you vaguely remember from sophomore year. Their language is quieter, deeper, and annoyingly subtle at times. They often speak simply through nudges, impressions, and emotions, and it takes practice to read them.

A Quick Note Before We Dive In

There are countless ways to communicate with your spirit guides. These are simply the ones that have worked best for me. They are the methods I return to again and again because they feel natural, grounded, and effective. You may discover your own variations or entirely different techniques that fit your personality better. Perfect. Your relationship with your spirit guides is meant to be personal, not standardized. Take what resonates and trust yourself to shape the rest.

Intuition — Your Spirit Guides' Native Language

If spirit guides had a mother tongue, intuition would be it. Intuition is that flash of insight you didn't "reason" your way into. It's the feeling in your chest that says yes long before your mind has caught up. It's the tiny tug that pulls your attention to something you would have missed otherwise. Intuition isn't loud, and it isn't dramatic, but it is consistent. Once you start recognizing it as a form of communication rather than a random feeling, everything changes.

Your spirit guides send intuitive messages the way the sun sends warmth. It is constant, effortless, and doesn't require you to perform a ritual every time. The challenge is that intuition often feels similar to your own thoughts.

That's the design. Your spirit guides don't hijack your mind or override your personality. They work through you, not around you. So when you have a question or concern about something on your mind, then get a sudden idea that hits with a soft but unmistakable weight… that's them. When you keep thinking about the same option over and over for reasons you can't quite explain… that's them again.

Learning to "talk" to your spirit guides means learning to understand this intuitive language. The good news is you already speak it. You're fluent. You've been fluent since you were a kid. We just have to remind you how to notice it again.

Writing — An Easy Doorway In

If you want a low-pressure, zero-embarrassment way to talk to your spirit guides, writing is the perfect starting point. It's private, it's quiet, and you don't have to worry about feeling ridiculous because… well, it's only you, your notebook, and a pen. No witnesses. No audience. Your ego doesn't get nearly as loud when your mouth stays shut.

Journaling with your spirit guides works because it slows your mind down enough for intuition to seep through the cracks. When you think internally, thoughts zip by like cars on a freeway. When you write, everything has to pass through the one-lane road of your pen. That gives your spirit guides way more space to slip their answers in.

Here is the method I use, and it is incredibly simple: Write your question. Literally write it on the page. "What do I need to know today?" or "What's the next right step?" or "Why am I feeling anxious?" Anything.

Then write their answer. Don't overthink it. Don't wait for fireworks. Just start writing whatever comes to mind.

Even if it feels as if you're making it up, keep going. Your intuition needs a runway, and this is how it gets it.

Optional (but highly recommended for fun): Use different colored pens. Lots of people, including me, find it helpful to write their words in one color and the spirit guides' response in another. It visually separates the voices and signals your brain, "Okay, we're shifting modes now." Does it look a little whimsical? Sure. Does it work? Absolutely. As you do this more often, something amazing happens. Your spirit guides' "voice" starts feeling distinct from your everyday thoughts. It's calmer, wiser, and much kinder (and sometimes a little cheeky). It doesn't rush, doesn't panic, and it often says things you needed to hear but wouldn't have phrased that way yourself.

The key is consistency, not perfection. If one day your writing feels muddy and unsure, keep going. If the next day it flows as if you're transcribing something whispered into your ear, enjoy that too. Every session strengthens the connection, builds trust, and teaches your intuition how to stretch its legs.

Meditation — But Not the Kind You're Thinking Of

Let's get one thing out of the way right now. You do not need to sit cross-legged on a Himalayan mountaintop to talk to your spirit guides. In fact, if the word meditation immediately makes you picture yourself failing to clear your mind while your grocery list screams for attention… congratulations, you're normal. A lot of people resist this idea because meditation has been marketed like an elite athletic event: no thoughts, perfect posture, serene expression, and zero twitches allowed. That's not what we're doing here. When it comes to communicating with your spirit guides, meditation isn't about becoming thoughtless. It's about becoming quiet enough inside that you can hear the conversation beneath the noise.

This is not regular intuition. Regular intuition is fast, subtle, and often shows up in the middle of your life while you're doing something else. Meditation is intentionally carving out a moment to listen. It's you turning toward the connection instead of waiting for it to tap you on the shoulder while you're folding laundry. A simple way to start:

Sit comfortably on a couch, your bed, a recliner, or maybe a patio chair while your dog watches you as if you've lost your mind. Anything goes.

Close your eyes. You're not trying to empty your mind. You're turning down the volume. Think "dim the lights," not "power outage."

Bring their presence to mind. Imagine sitting across from your spirit guides or beside them or sensing them nearby. I personally sit in a circle with them. You don't need to visualize anything dramatic. Even a vague "someone's here" feeling counts.

Ask a single question. One, not twelve, not your entire life plan, just something simple such as, "What do you want me to know right now?"

Then listen for the answer. Here's the trick. You're not listening for words. You're listening for a shift, a calming, or a new thought that drifts in like it was already halfway formed. A feeling that settles in your chest. That's the response.

Meditation doesn't make the spirit guides speak louder. It helps you get quieter. It gives their answers somewhere to settle instead of bouncing off a stressed-out mind that's juggling a thousand to-do items. And if you can only sit quietly for thirty seconds before your brain reminds you of that sock you left in the dryer, that's great. Thirty seconds is plenty. Your spirit guides aren't grading you. This isn't Meditation Olympics. This is you showing up with honest intention, and that's all they need.

Conversations Through Signs

If writing feels easy and meditation feels challenging, sign-based communication is the perfect middle ground. It's active, it's playful, and it lets your spirit guides respond in the physical world where your logical brain can't easily dismiss it. Remember all that work we did back in the signs chapter? This is where it pays off because talking through signs is really only continuing a conversation you already started. The key is this: Signs are not random when you ask for them on purpose. When you make a clear request, your spirit guides have something specific to work with and they love that. Here's how to do it:

Ask a specific question. Not "Should I change my entire life?" Try: "Is this job opportunity aligned?" or "Is this friendship healthy for me?" or "Do you support me moving forward with this idea?"

Assign the sign. Pick something that won't blend into the scenery. A repeated number sequence, a heart shape in the wild, or a certain animal. Maybe a song or a phrase. Anything that will stand out to you.

Give them a timeframe. Not to boss them around, but to give you clarity. "If this is the right direction, show me a white feather in the next forty-eight hours." It keeps the answer from becoming a vague someday event.

Then, the hardest part, go live your life. Don't stare at the sky waiting for a cloud to arrange itself into a heart. Don't refresh your playlist hoping for the right song. Go about your day. Let the spirit guides be in charge of delivery.

When the sign appears, it won't feel random anymore. It will hit you with that there-it-is sense. A little jolt of recognition. Talking to your spirit guides through signs isn't about magical thinking. It's about clarity, intention, and giving the universe a visible way to answer. It works because you're engaging your intuition and the world around you, bridging the seen and the unseen.

Pendulums & Cards — Tools, Not Magic Tricks

Okay, deep breath. We're stepping one inch further into the mystical pool… but let's keep our feet firmly on the ground. Pendulums, tarot cards, and oracle decks are not "fortune-telling devices." They are communication tools. Think of them as spiritual translators who help you access guidance you're already receiving but may not yet trust. These tools don't override your free will, and they don't summon shadowy beings from the underworld. They help you bypass your thinking brain so you can hear the quieter layers underneath. They are nothing more than intuition amplifiers.

Think of pendulums as your yes/no hotline. If you aren't familiar, a pendulum is essentially a weighted object that moves in response to micro-signals from your subconscious, which, by the way, is one of your spirit guides' favorite doorways. They love it when you use a pendulum because it gives them a simple, physical way to nudge a message through. You ask a question. You hold the chain still. You let the movement answer.

Is it you? Is it them? It's both. Your subconscious is the bridge your spirit guides use, and the pendulum simply makes the message visible. It's not spooky. It's physics plus intuition. Pendulums are perfect for fast clarity, especially on small or emotionally tangled questions where you can't tell what you actually want. They're the spiritual version of texting your best friend, "Okay, just tell me yes or no before I spiral."

Tarot and oracle cards are nothing but dialogue in picture form. They go one layer deeper than pendulums because they open a full conversation instead of a single answer. They give you images, themes, archetypes, and emotional tones. They give you context. They help you see what's influencing a situation and where your energy is flowing. People often think the cards "predict" something, but really they're showing you what you're feeling, what you're afraid of, what your intuition already knows, and where your spirit guides are nudging you.

The beauty of tarot and oracle cards is that your spirit guides work through your interpretation. They highlight certain words. They make an image stand out. They help a metaphor click. It feels like the deck is speaking, but truly, your spirit guides are using the cards as flashcards for your intuition. Here's the best part. You don't have to be a mystical expert to use them. You don't need to remember what the Seven of Cups means from memory (trust me, ninety-nine percent of us peek at the guidebook). Simply pull a card, look at it, and ask, "What are you trying to show me?"

When you treat cards and pendulums as extensions of your own inner knowing, not magical props, they become powerful, reliable tools in the ongoing conversation between you and your spirit team.

Common Mistakes When Talking to Your Spirit Guides

Even the most intuitive, spiritually-tuned humans trip over the same handful of pitfalls when they start communicating with their spirit guides. These aren't character flaws. They're simply habits we learned from living in a world that worships logic and side-eyes anything subtle or internal. So if you catch yourself doing any of these, welcome. You're human. You're in great company.

Number one: expecting the answer to sound like a boom mic from heaven. If you're waiting for a Morgan Freeman voice from the sky declaring your destiny… yeah, that's Hollywood, not spirituality. Spirit guides don't shout. They don't broadcast. They don't override your mind. Their communication slides in gently, as a quiet idea, a soft knowing, and a feeling that settles instead of argues. If your expectation is too dramatic, you'll miss the steady, reliable ways they're already answering.

Number two: asking twelve questions at once. Spirit guides love you deeply, but they're not trying to take the SAT with you. When you rapid-fire questions such as: Should I quit my job? Should I stay? Should I switch careers? Should I move? Should I cut my bangs? Should I buy a dog? …you create static. It's similar to trying to catch one radio station while spinning the dial nonstop. Ask one question. Receive. Then ask the next. Your clarity gives their guidance room to reach you.

Number three: ignoring the first answer because you don't agree with it. Okay, this one is me. Your spirit guides will often give you the simplest, clearest answer right away, and your ego will immediately jump in to make you think that answer can't possibly be it. If the message feels straightforward, calm, and quietly certain… it's probably them. If your brain argues? That's you. You don't have to obey every message as if it's a court order, but don't pretend you "didn't get one" only because it didn't say what you wanted. We've all been there. Zero judgment.

Number four: treating your spirit guides as if they are customer service. Your spirit guides aren't here to provide tracking updates on the package of your destiny. They don't respond to demanding energy, ultimatums, or emotional ransom notes. ("If you want me to follow your path, show me a raccoon in the next ten minutes!") They respond to collaboration, openness, curiosity, and willingness. They're partners, not cosmic employees.

Number five: expecting communication to feel the same every time. Some days your connection feels crystal clear. Other days it's like trying to hear a whisper through a snowstorm. This doesn't mean they left you. It means your energy, mood, or mental clutter shifted. Spiritual communication is fluid. It evolves. Sometimes your spirit guides are working behind the scenes in ways you can't feel yet. The biggest mistake you can make is assuming the connection is broken when it's simply changing.

Before You Go

Talking to your spirit guides isn't something you master. It's something you grow into bit by bit and day by day. Some moments will feel effortless, as if you're tuning into a familiar voice you forgot you knew. Others will feel clumsy or quiet, and that's okay. Connection isn't built through perfection. It's built through showing up, trying again, and trusting the small openings when they appear. Your spirit guides don't need you to be confident. They don't need you to be psychic, serene, or spiritually impressive. They just need your willingness. Every question you ask, every sign you notice, every tiny whisper you follow, it all strengthens the bridge between you and them.

So be patient with yourself. Be curious. Be brave in the gentle, steady ways that only you can be. And remember, you're not doing this alone. You've never been doing this alone. Every step you take toward communication is met with a step toward you. As you get more comfortable talking to your spirit guides, something naturally begins to shift. Communication turns into collaboration. Questions turn into movement. You start to notice that guidance isn't only about answers. It's about creation. Every nudge, every intuitive yes, every moment of willingness becomes part of a quiet partnership between you and your spirit guides.

In the next chapter, we'll explore how that partnership expands into manifestation, and how co-creating with your spirit guides works in real, grounded ways that don't require perfection, only intention, trust, and follow through.

11

Manifesting Basics: Co-Creating with Your Spirit Guides

Manifesting isn't about snapping your fingers and suddenly having your dream house, your perfect job, and a mystical girlfriend appear out of nowhere. (I mean… fun, but no.) Manifesting is really about partnership. You, your energy, your choices, and your spirit guides working together in a steady, intentional rhythm. When you understand this collaboration, everything starts to move with a little more ease, a little more magic, and a whole lot more direction.

Most people think manifesting is "wishful thinking on steroids," but that's like saying baking is "putting flour in a bowl." It's technically part of the process, but you're missing the butter, sugar, heat, and the patience not to open the oven door too early. Manifesting is a full-body, full-spirit experience. A way of showing the cosmos what you're ready for and then allowing your spirit guides to help you build toward it.

What Manifesting Actually Is (Beyond the Clichés)

Manifesting, at its core, is intentional alignment. You

are lining up your energy, beliefs, actions, and expectations with what you want to bring into your life. It's the process of getting crystal clear about what you want, holding the emotional frequency of already having it, then taking aligned actions that move you toward it. You let your spirit guides remove obstacles, redirect you, or speed things up while staying receptive rather than gripping the outcome as if you are a raccoon with a shiny object.

Here's the part that most people skip. You have to tell your spirit guides what you're trying to create. They respond to your clarity, your willingness, and the way you communicate, whether that's through journaling, meditation, signs, or simply speaking your intentions out loud in your car like a slightly eccentric but lovable human.

When you loop your spirit guides in, your manifesting work becomes a conversation rather than a silent wish. You're not just hoping something happens, you're coordinating with the very team that can orchestrate synchronicities, strengthen your intuition, and nudge you toward the right people and opportunities. When people say, "thoughts become things," what they really mean is your thoughts guide your focus, your focus shapes your actions, your actions create momentum, and your spirit guides take that momentum and amplify it.

Manifesting is a co-creation, not a solo performance. Your spirit guides can open doors, nudge you toward opportunities, and strengthen your intuition, but you are the one signaling what you're ready to receive. You bring clarity, willingness, and action. They bring the support, synchronicities, and step-by-step guidance. Together? You build the life you want, not through force, but through alignment.

Simple First Steps: Intention, Attention, and Alignment

Manifesting can look complicated from the outside, but the foundation is beautifully simple. Everything begins with three core steps. Think of it as your manifesting starter kit: intention, attention, and alignment.

Intention is the "what." It's you deciding what you want to create, experience, receive, or become. Your spirit guides can help you refine it, but the spark comes from you. Intention is your declaration that this is the direction you're choosing.

Attention is the "focus." Where your mind goes, your energy follows. What you consistently pay attention to grows stronger in your awareness and more present in your energy field. Attention is how you water the seed you planted with intention. You do it daily, gently, and without obsessively digging it up to see if it's sprouting yet.

Alignment is the "matching." This is where your actions, energy, and beliefs start to line up with what you're manifesting. If intention is the wish and attention is the focus, alignment is the embodiment. It's how you show your spirit guides, "I'm ready. I'm serious. I'm becoming the person who lives this reality."

You don't have to be perfect. You don't have to feel radiant or enlightened or tuned like a singing bowl. You simply start making choices, small ones, that match where you want to go instead of where you've been. This is the moment your spirit guides lean in. Because once you're taking even tiny, aligned steps, they can amplify your efforts and smooth the path ahead.

Your First Aligned Step

Let's turn this into something tangible.

1. *Intention*: Write down one thing you want to manifest. Something simple, small, and immediate. Not the dream house or the huge life overhaul. Just something real and relevant. Examples: finally paying off that one stubborn bill, meeting someone new and meaningful, or landing a small but needed financial win.

2. *Attention*: List two ways you can keep this intention in your awareness without obsessing over it. Maybe you put a reminder on your fridge, say a quick thank you to your spirit guides each morning, or take a moment in the car to re-center on what you're calling in.

3. *Alignment*: Identify one tiny action you can take today that matches that intention. If you're manifesting paying a bill, maybe you double-check your bank account transactions. If you're manifesting meeting someone special, maybe you say yes to a social invitation. If it's a financial win, maybe you follow an intuitive nudge to apply for something you've been putting off. You're not trying to "make it happen." You're signaling readiness, and that's all your spirit guides need to start meeting you halfway.

Why Trying Too Hard Backfires

One of the sneakiest ways people sabotage their manifesting is by gripping their desires so tightly they practically strangle the energy. When you try too hard by pushing, forcing, obsessing, or refreshing your email every ten minutes "just to check," you shift out of creation and straight into desperation. Desperate energy is spiritual bug spray. Your spirit guides can still reach you, but it makes everything a little harder than it needs to be.

Trying too hard usually comes from fear. You worry about things such as "*What if this doesn't happen?*" or *"What if I mess it up?"* or *"What if the spirit guides forgot about me?"* But here's the thing. When you're attempting to manifest from a place of fear or scarcity, your energy gets tight. Your focus narrows. You stop listening to your intuition and start micromanaging every detail like a cosmic control freak. And your spirit guides? They're standing there sending, "Hey, we've got this, but you've got to give us a little room to work."

Manifesting is a collaboration, not a hostage negotiation. If you're trying to manhandle the outcome, you're essentially saying you don't trust the timing, the guidance, or the quiet nudges that are meant to lead you there. The more you push, the more you create anxiety instead of clarity, resistance instead of flow, and overthinking instead of intuitive openness. That "I must make this happen now" energy doesn't match the reality you're trying to call in. You can't manifest ease from tension. You can't manifest abundance from panic. You can't manifest love from fear of being alone. It's like trying to water a plant with a fire hose. Technically, it's water, but things get messy fast.

Letting go doesn't mean giving up. It means you loosen your grip enough to let your spirit guides participate. Think of it similar to holding a kite. You guide it, you stay connected, but if you yank the string constantly, it nosedives. When you give it enough slack, it flies. Trying hard is fine. Caring is fine. Taking aligned action is fabulous. It's the over-trying that shuts the door you're trying to open. Trust, space, and a little breathing room aren't luxuries in manifesting. They're part of the mechanism.

How to Stay Open Without Losing Enthusiasm

Staying open while still caring deeply about what you're manifesting is a balancing act, and one your spirit guides are more than happy to help you with. You don't have to detach from your desires or pretend you don't care. You simply have to hold them in a way that feels spacious rather than strained. One of the best ways to stay open is to keep reconnecting to the feeling of your desire instead of the outcome itself. You can enjoy the anticipation, savor the idea, smile at the thought of what's coming, without demanding it arrive on your schedule. When you focus on the feeling, your energy stays soft, and your trust stays intact.

Another way is to remind yourself that your spirit guides are working behind the scenes in ways you absolutely cannot see yet. Just because you haven't spotted the path doesn't mean it's not being cleared. That little reminder that they're on it keeps enthusiasm alive without tipping into obsession. Staying open also means giving your intention room to evolve. Sometimes a better version of your desire is waiting in the wings. If you stay curious rather than controlling, you make space for delightful surprises. You're still playing the game, but you're not trying to call every single shot. And finally, keep living your life while the manifestation is in motion. Enjoy the day you're in. Do things that light you up. Talk to your spirit guides, dance in the kitchen, or take a walk. Enthusiasm thrives when you're rooted in the present instead of hovering anxiously in the "what if."

Celebrate the Breadcrumbs

One of the easiest ways to stay open without drifting

into impatience is to celebrate the breadcrumbs. These are the small signs that your manifestation is already taking shape. They are tiny moments that don't always look like the outcome itself, but they're proof the energy is shifting and your spirit guides are quietly setting the table.

If you're manifesting paying off a bill, a breadcrumb might be an unexpected discount, a small refund check, or even finding a few dollars on the sidewalk. None of those pay the bill by themselves, but they show movement. They show alignment. They show access points your spirit guides can expand. If you're manifesting meeting someone special, a breadcrumb could be a great conversation with a stranger, a friend inviting you somewhere you normally wouldn't go, or even feeling a tiny spark of confidence you haven't felt in a while. These small glimmers mean your energy is changing, and when your energy changes, your experiences follow.

Breadcrumbs keep your enthusiasm alive because they show you the path is active even when the destination isn't visible yet. They remind you that manifesting isn't an overnight event. It's a series of nudges, hints, and little "we're on it" messages from your spirit guides. Every time you pause to notice and appreciate one, you deepen your openness, strengthen your trust, and help your spirit guides keep the momentum going.

A Real-Life Breadcrumb Moment

Here's a small example from my own life. Recently, I'd been quietly manifesting a little more financial breathing room. Nothing dramatic. Just asking my spirit guides to help me stretch my monthly budget. One day I got the nudge to fill out a form related to my expenses. I wasn't confident anything would come of it, but I listened to the tug and did it anyway. A couple of weeks passed, and then a letter arrived in the mail with information I wasn't expecting. I set it aside at first, assuming I'd misunderstood it, but later on I sat down, read it carefully, and realized it might be real. I double-checked it, fully prepared for it to be a mistake, but it wasn't. The change it brought freed up hundreds of dollars each month and is exactly the kind of ease I'd been hoping for. For a full-time author, where every penny counts, that breathing room felt like a hug from my spirit guides.

It didn't start with the big moment, though. It started with breadcrumbs. The nudge to fill out the form. The quiet feeling that I should at least try. The letter arriving on a day I almost didn't check the mail. It reminded me that our spirit guides often work quietly and steadily, and the magic is already in motion long before we realize something is about to shift.

As you practice co-creating with your spirit guides, you may start to notice that the guidance feels easier to catch. The breadcrumbs stand out a little more. The nudges feel clearer, quicker, and harder to ignore. That's not coincidence, it's responsiveness. The more you engage in this partnership, the more attuned you become to how your spirit guides communicate with you. In the next chapter, we'll focus on how to strengthen that attunement and turn up the volume on your connection, so the guidance you're already receiving becomes even easier to recognize, trust, and follow.

12

Turning Up the Volume on Your Connection

Some days your intuition comes in loud and clear. Think of it as a friend yelling across a parking lot because you left your coffee on the roof again. Other days? It's more like a whisper drifting through a thick fog. The truth is, your spirit guides aren't whispering. You've just been busy being wonderfully, beautifully human, and that's okay. With a few gentle shifts and a little intentional awareness, you can tune in more easily and start catching those messages that are already floating your way.

Tiny Daily Habits That Strengthen the Channel

Strengthening your connection doesn't require a mountaintop, a robe, or the ability to sit cross-legged without something cramping. It's built through tiny daily rituals, through easy, practical things you can do between emails, errands, and feeding the dog. These micro-moments create consistency, and consistency creates clarity. Here are some habits that gently deepen the channel.

Try one conscious breath. Only one. In and out. Feel

your body relax and notice that a tiny pause creates a pocket of stillness your spirit guides can slip into. You can also try a quick hello. As simple as "Good morning, spirit guides," or "Hey, I'm here." It's the metaphysical equivalent of turning your phone off airplane mode.

Take a moment to notice the world around you. A bird landing on the railing, the way your coffee smells, or the flicker of a thought that feels different. These moments sharpen your awareness, and awareness is the foundation of connection. A ten-second gratitude check can really help. Not a giant list, only one thing. Gratitude increases your energetic "receptivity," which your spirit guides love to work with. Along with that, try an end-of-day reflection. A tiny one. "Where did I feel guided today?" Nothing formal (although journaling is great too). Just a soft look back. You'll be surprised how much you catch.

Don't be shy about sending out a micro-ask. "What's my next step?" or "Help me stay calm today." Small, clear asks prime the channel and remind you you're not doing life alone. These habits work because they tether your awareness to the present moment, and the present moment is where your spirit guides already are, waving politely.

Energy Hygiene and Emotional Clearing

Your intuition works best when your inner space isn't packed wall-to-wall with stress, worry, resentment, or that one conversation you keep replaying because you wish you had thought of that witty comeback (which came to you a minute after you walked away). Energy hygiene isn't about being perfect or Zen all the time, it's about giving your system enough room to breathe so your spirit guides can get a word in edgewise. Think of it as clearing off a cluttered kitchen counter. You don't need to deep-clean the whole house. You simply need some space to chop the veggies.

One thing to try is a quick emotional check-in. Take ten seconds and examine what's truly going on inside you. Naming emotions loosens their grip. Recognizing you're overwhelmed or tired and bringing it into awareness shifts your energy.

Movement is great to reset your field too. You don't need a workout. Shake out your hands, roll your shoulders, or stand up and stretch like a cat who owns the place (I have three, so I know how that looks). A little movement knocks loose stagnant energy. There is also the two-breath reset. One breath in to invite clarity. One breath out to release what's heavy. Done. No incense required.

Try letting one thing go. Not everything, just one thing. One worry you don't have to solve right now. One grudge you can set on the shelf. One "what if" you can drop for the next hour (or forever). Space opens fast when you loosen even a single knot.

A light sweep of your environment works wonders too. Energy collects in places like your workspace, your bedroom, or under the seat of your car where old receipts go to die. Opening a window, straightening a stack of books, or lighting a candle shifts the atmosphere enough to help you feel clearer.

Most importantly, find compassion for yourself. This is the secret sauce. Harsh self-talk muddies the channel faster than anything. A little kindness toward yourself clears it better than sage ever could. You don't have to walk around glowing like a rose quartz tower. Just a few intentional resets a day keep your inner landscape open, steady, and ready for guidance.

What to Do When Guidance Feels Quiet

Every intuitive path has quiet stretches. It's not because your spirit guides wandered off for a snack break, but because life gets loud. Responsibilities stack up, emotions get tangled, and your mind turns into a crowded room where nothing can be heard clearly. When that happens, it's easy to jump to the conclusion that something is wrong with you or your connection. But quiet doesn't mean absence. It only means the signal needs a little space.

When everything feels still, the first step is to stop pushing. Straining to see or hear something only tightens the channel. Instead, take a moment to breathe and let the silence be what it is. Your spirit guides often speak in subtle ways, and pressure turns subtle into invisible. Then, shift your attention to the world around you. Guidance often comes through the small things you're tempted to overlook. Something such as a thought that feels gentler than your own inner voice, a memory that pops up out of nowhere, or the sudden urge to choose a different route home. When you can't hear anything inside, look outward. Let your environment speak for a while.

Another powerful move is to bring your body into the conversation. Clarity returns quickly when you rest, hydrate, or step outside for three minutes of fresh air. The physical world is one of your spirit guides' favorite communication tools. They'll often nudge you toward something that calms your nervous system so you can feel them again. And finally, trust the rhythm. Intuition has tides. Some days are high flow, and others are low tide. Nothing has gone wrong. In the quiet, your system is recalibrating, and preparing for the next wave of clarity. The silence isn't a void. It's a reset. Let it work for you, and your guidance will return, usually quieter at first… then unmistakable.

Reset & Retune Moment

Find a comfortable spot, nothing fancy. You don't need candles, crystals, or a perfectly quiet room, only a moment to yourself. Sit, stand, flop onto the couch… whatever works.

Start by placing a hand over your chest or your stomach, whichever spot feels most "home" to your body. Take one slow breath in and imagine your spirit guides doing the same breath right alongside you. As you exhale, picture the static inside you clearing, like a radio fading back into focus.

Now, close your eyes for a moment and ask one simple question: "Where do I now feel calmer in my body?" Don't go hunting for a profound answer. Just notice the first tiny spark. Maybe your left shoulder softened, or your belly relaxed half an inch, or maybe your pinky toe feels strangely serene. That tiny point of calm is your anchor.

Breathe into that spot as if it's a warm ember you're helping glow brighter. With each inhale, imagine the ember expanding a little. With each exhale, imagine it dissolving tension around it. You're resetting your entire energetic field with micro-moments of calm.

When you're ready, gently ask, "What do you need me to know right now?" Don't force an answer. It might be an image, a word, a feeling, or even simply a sense of peaceful blankness. The reset has already happened. The channel is clearer and you're back in tune.

How to Rebuild Connection After Doubt

Doubt has a sneaky way of convincing you it has ruined everything. One wobble, one moment of second-guessing, one "Did I imagine all of this?" and suddenly it feels like the whole bridge between you and your spirit guides collapsed into the river. But doubt doesn't break your connection, it just scrambles the signal for a moment. Kind of similar to someone suddenly standing between you and the TV when you're trying to watch the baseball game (Go, Dodgers).

The most important thing you can do is stop treating doubt as a personal failure. Doubt is normal. It's human. It shows up whenever you're stretching into something meaningful. The real magic isn't in never doubting… It's in what you do after. Start by acknowledging it without judgment. That alone loosens the grip. Doubt thrives in secrecy, and it shrinks the moment you drag it into the light.

Then, reconnect in the simplest, gentlest way you can. Don't try to force a big spiritual moment or demand a sign on command. Instead, go back to the basics. Go back to one breath, one hello, or one tiny intention that you're opening up again. Connection rebuilds through gentleness, not pressure. It also helps to remember that your spirit guides don't get offended when you doubt. They don't roll their eyes or wander off in frustration. They wait patiently for the fog to clear, because they know the truth of who you are underneath the noise. They know you will always find your way back.

Here's the part doubt never wants you to realize. Coming back after a wobble usually deepens your connection, not weakens it. Every time you return, reopen, retrust, and retune, you grow steadier and stronger. You become more confident in what you're feeling. Doubt slows the path for a moment, but it never locks the door. All you have to do is reach for the handle again.

Recognizing Your "Yes," "No," and "Not Yet" Signals

Your spirit guides are constantly answering you, but they don't usually shout "YES!" or "ABSOLUTELY NOT, MY FRIEND." Instead, they speak through your body, your emotions, your thoughts, and those subtle shifts in energy that you've felt a thousand times without knowing what they were. Your personal intuitive signals are already there. Your job is simply to notice what's been true for you all along.

A "yes" often feels similar to expansion. A lift in the chest. A breath that flows more easily. It can feel like warmth, or curiosity, or a feeling of rightness that doesn't need explaining. Sometimes it's that spark of excitement that pops up before the mind has a chance to list all the reasons something is impractical. "Yes" usually comes across as forward motion, even if it's gentle.

A "no" tends to sit differently. It feels heavier, tighter, or suddenly complicated. You may feel pressure in your head, tension in your stomach, or a subtle urge to back away. Sometimes it shows up as immediate disinterest or irritation you can't logically justify. The answer "no" often feels as if your body is leaning away, even if you're physically still.

Then there's the trickiest one: "not yet." This one rarely gets the credit it deserves. It isn't a rejection. It's timing. "Not yet" can feel like a mixed message. Part of you is drawn to something, but you also feel resistance or fogginess around it. You might feel tired when you think about taking action, or the path ahead looks blurry instead of clear. Nothing is wrong… it's just not time.

Learning these signals is similar to learning a language you've secretly spoken your whole life. The fastest way is to pay attention in real time. When someone invites you to something, when a decision lands in your lap, or when an idea flickers in your mind, don't think first. Feel first. Your body reacts long before your brain kicks in with commentary. Over time, you'll start noticing patterns. The same sensations show up again and again. Once you know your signals, decision-making becomes clearer, faster, and a whole lot less dramatic. Your spirit guides are always giving you the green light, the red light, or the gentle yellow, and now you're learning how to read the signals.

Making Connection a Natural Part of Your Day

The easiest way to stay connected with your spirit guides is to stop treating connection as if it were an appointment. You don't have to wait for the perfect moment, the perfect meditation, or the stars to align as if they're trying to impress you. Your spirit guides fit into your day the same way sunlight shines through your windows. It is effortless, quiet, and doesn't need permission.

Connection becomes natural when you fold it into the little in-between spaces. Saying hello while you make your morning coffee. Asking a quick question when you're standing in line at the grocery store (probably in your head, you know, that whole sounding bananas thing). Pausing before you open your email to see what your intuition nudges you toward first. Letting a quiet moment in the car or shower be a chance to check in rather than zone out. It's less about adding something new and more about gently tuning into what's already happening. The more often you reach out, with even tiny acknowledgments, the more familiar the rhythm becomes. Before long, you won't be trying to connect at all. You'll be moving through your day with a subtle awareness that you're supported, guided, and never on your own.

That's the goal. Connection woven so lightly into your routines that it is second nature. You don't have to be perfect. You only have to be willing, and every small moment of willingness adds up to a channel that stays open without effort. As your connection settles into something steady and familiar, guidance naturally stops feeling as if it's a special event and starts feeling like part of everyday life. The conversation isn't reserved for quiet moments or big decisions anymore. It weaves itself into ordinary choices, passing thoughts, and daily rhythms. In the next chapter, we'll focus on how to keep that connection active and reciprocal, turning guidance into a true two-way street where listening, responding, and trusting become part of how you move through the world.

13

Everyday Guidance: Make It a Two-Way Street

There's a moment, usually somewhere between the first signs and the first big manifestation, when you realize your spirit guides aren't only background characters in your spiritual life. They're active participants. They're collaborators. They're basically the friends who answer your texts before you've even finished typing them. Once you notice that, something shifts. Guidance stops being a once-in-a-while event and becomes an easy, natural part of your day.

Asking for Clarity or Confirmation

Let's be honest. Sometimes guidance feels like a whisper drifting through a hurricane. You think you heard something… maybe… but also, maybe that was your stomach growling. Here's the good news. Your spirit guides don't need you to pretend you're confident when you're not. They love it when you ask for clarity. A simple, "I'm not sure I understood, can you repeat that?" works beautifully. It's the spiritual equivalent of asking someone to speak up in a crowded room. You're not doubting them. You're making sure you caught the message correctly.

You can absolutely ask for confirmation. Not in a "prove it to me now" way, but in a gentle, collaborative way. If you're torn between two choices, ask for help making the clearer path stand out. Your spirit guides aren't offended. They're relieved you're inviting them into the conversation instead of trying to decode everything solo. Think of it as asking a friend for a second opinion.

For example, maybe you get the nudge to reach out to someone you haven't talked to in ages. You feel the pull, but part of you wonders if you're imagining it. So you ask your spirit guides, "If this is really from you, can you nudge me again in a way I'll notice?" Then later that day you randomly see that person's first name on a billboard, or they comment on your social media post, or you stumble across an old photo on your phone of the two of you. That's confirmation. Not forced, not hunted for, just naturally showing up in your path.

Using Signs to Navigate Decisions

Signs get a bad rap sometimes. They're either treated like cosmic scavenger hunts or as mysterious riddles you're supposed to solve before midnight. But that's not what they're for. A sign isn't a puzzle. It's a nudge, a gentle suggestion, or a little "psst, over here" from your spirit guides. When you're facing a decision, big or small, you can ask for a sign to help illuminate the clearer direction. And the key word really is illuminate. Signs don't override your free will or rewrite your life plan. They simply light up the path that already feels most aligned. They make the choice easier to notice, not harder. The best signs are simple and unmistakable. If you ask for guidance and suddenly start seeing repeating numbers, or the same symbol three times in one day, or someone says the exact phrase you were thinking about, those aren't coincidences you have to squint at sideways. Those are breadcrumbs your spirit guides dropped right in front of you.

Let's say you're trying to choose between two projects. Both look fine on paper, but something about one feels ever-so-slightly more "you," even though you can't articulate why. You ask your spirit guides, "If the one I'm leaning toward is the right one, give me a sign I can't miss." Later that afternoon, you see the project title on a poster in the hall that you walk through every day but never noticed before. The sign doesn't tell you what to decide. It simply boosts the volume on the option your intuition was already whispering about.

If you get nothing? No problem. That's a sign too. It simply means either choice is fine or, occasionally, that the timing isn't right yet. Signs are partners in clarity, not pressure. The magic is in staying open, relaxed, and curious. Signs love to show up for people who aren't hunting for them.

Creating Daily Check-In Rituals

Let's pause for a second, because the word "ritual" can sound intense, like you need candles, chanting, and a dramatic robe. Not here. A daily check-in with your spirit guides is simply a small moment of connection, the same way you might text good morning to a friend or glance at your emails before starting the day. These tiny check-ins are the secret to making your relationship with your spirit guides feel steady and natural. You're not asking for big revelations every time. You're simply opening the door. Here's the best part. The more often you open that door, the easier it becomes to sense them in all the noise of your day.

Your check-in doesn't have to happen at the same time or in the same way. Maybe it's while your coffee brews. Maybe it's the moment before you open your laptop. Maybe it's the thirty seconds during your morning walk when you simply ask, "Anything I should know today?" It doesn't need ceremony, only presence. Next time, try this. Imagine you sit down for the morning, take a deep breath, and say, "I'm here. I'm listening." That's it. No fanfare. Later, you notice you're more patient than usual, or a thought pops into your mind about something that needs attention, or you get a burst of clarity about where to focus your energy. That wasn't a coincidence. That was your spirit guides answering the door you opened hours earlier.

Daily check-ins aren't about perfection. They're about consistency. You're building a relationship, not taking attendance. Some days you'll feel a spark. Some days you won't. Both are completely normal. What matters is showing up in small, steady, easy ways that remind your spirit guides that you're ready and you're open.

A Five-Day Check-In Practice

If you want to deepen this even more, here's a gentle little experiment. Nothing dramatic. Simply a way to help your intuition and your spirit guides learn each other's rhythms. For the next five days, set one special moment each morning to pause and check in. It can be while the coffee drips, while you're brushing your teeth, or even sitting in your car before you start the engine. Keep it extremely simple. Place a hand on your heart or stomach, take a single, slower breath and say, silently or out loud:

"Good morning. I'm here. Anything I should know today?"

Then go about your day normally. No hovering, no waiting for lightning bolts, no over-analyzing every passing cloud shaped as a penguin. At the end of each day, jot down one thing that felt like guidance. Maybe you saw a hummingbird appear out of nowhere or heard a bell sound when no obvious bell was nearby or a random song lyric that fit what you needed to hear a little too perfectly. If nothing comes to mind, write that down too. Blank space is part of the dialogue.

By day five, you'll notice something: you're not "trying" to connect anymore. You're simply open and that openness makes the conversations with your spirit guides smoother, easier, and far more natural.

Letting Guidance Help with Simple Choices

One of the easiest ways to strengthen your connection with your spirit guides is to let them into the tiny, ordinary decisions you make every day. We tend to think guidance is reserved for the big crossroads. Things like changing careers, moving states, or signing contracts. But your spirit guides are constantly whispering in the small spaces too. Those small spaces are actually where your intuition gets the best practice.

Simple choices are low-pressure. They let you tune in without fear of "getting it wrong." Think of them as warm-ups before the bigger decisions arrive. You can start with things such as whether you should take a walk now or later. Maybe have them help pick which route you should take home. Even have help deciding if you should reach out to that person who popped into your mind.

Imagine you're deciding between two grocery stores.

One is slightly out of the way, and one is on your usual path. There's no right or wrong answer here, but you get a little tug toward the out-of-the-way one. Nothing dramatic, just a gentle nudge. You follow it, and while you're there, you run into someone who gives you a piece of information you absolutely needed. That's guidance working through the mundane. Your spirit guides love these small choices because they help you build trust in your own inner signals. The more you practice listening when the stakes are low, the more natural it feels to listen when something important shows up.

Here's the real beauty. Once you start involving your spirit guides in these little decisions, your whole day becomes a collaboration with subtle nudges, gentle whispers, simple signs, and the occasional cosmic wink guiding you from task to task. It's not about asking permission for every move you make. It's about letting your intuition be part of the conversation in a way that feels friendly, supportive, and easy.

Balancing Intuition with Practicality

A lot of people secretly worry that once they start listening to their spirit guides, they'll have to toss their common sense into a drawer and make decisions solely on moonlight and goosebumps. Absolutely not. Your intuition isn't here to replace your logic. It's here to work with it. Think of intuition and practicality as two friends who balance each other. One sees the inner truth. The other sees the logistics. Your spirit guides don't expect you to ignore the very real details of your life. They love when you pair their nudges with grounded, thoughtful action.

Say you get a strong intuitive pull to explore a new job opportunity. Great. That nudge is the spark. But you still research the company and talk to people who've worked there. That's the practical part. Your spirit guides provide direction, and you provide the structure to walk the path. Or maybe your intuition says, "Take a break today," but your calendar says, "Hi, you have three meetings." Maybe the compromise is a ten-minute step outside between tasks instead of a full afternoon off. Listening to practicality doesn't mean you've failed spiritually. It means you're living a human life with human responsibilities. Guidance works with your reality, not against it.

Your spirit guides want you to be empowered, not reckless. They don't want you making every decision by throwing a feather in the air and seeing where it lands. They want you to combine their quiet wisdom with your experience, your instincts, and your very capable brain. The sweet spot is where intuition informs your choices and practicality shapes how you carry them out. When you treat them as teammates instead of rivals, everything starts to feel smoother, clearer, and a whole lot less dramatic.

Making the Relationship Feel Easy, Not Forced

One of the biggest misunderstandings about connecting with your spirit guides is the idea that you need to work hard at it. As if connection only counts when you're concentrating, meditating, visualizing, or doing something elaborate enough to make your cat stare at you funny. In reality, guidance shows up most clearly when you're relaxed, present, and not trying to force anything.

Think of your spirit guides as friends who love hanging out with you. They don't need you to show up in perfect spiritual form. They don't need drama or fanfare. They want you and your real-life, sometimes-distracted, occasionally-anxious, beautifully-human self. When you stop trying to perform spirituality, the relationship becomes lighter and far more authentic. If connection ever starts feeling like homework, that's your cue to ease off. Not quit. Just relax a little. Your spirit guides don't want you in that tight, effortful place. They want you curious, open, and comfortable. Imagine trying to have a deep conversation with someone who keeps thinking, *Am I doing this right? Am I doing it wrong? Are you sure you can hear me?* It's endearing, but it's also exhausting for both sides.

Guidance flows best when you let it. Don't chase it. Don't demand it. When you trust that your spirit guides are always there and that you don't have to "earn" their attention, the whole relationship becomes easier, more natural, and surprisingly joyful. Face it, you don't build a connection by trying harder. You build it by relaxing into what's already available. When the relationship feels easy, you're not doing something wrong. You're finally doing it right.

As everyday guidance becomes part of how you move through your life, the signs around you start to stand out more clearly. You're no longer wondering *if* guidance is happening. You're noticing *where* it's showing up. The symbols, patterns, and little coincidences that once felt easy to dismiss begin to feel intentional and timely. In the next chapter, we'll focus on how to follow those signs with confidence, understand what they're pointing you toward, and how to trust yourself when guidance starts appearing right in front of you.

14

Following the Signs

The moment you start noticing signs, the world shifts. Suddenly life feels a little more interactive, a little more enchanted, as if there's a quiet conversation happening beneath the surface of your day. But following those signs isn't about decoding every leaf that blows across your path. It's about learning to recognize what's truly meant for you, trusting what you sense, and building a relationship with guidance that feels steady and natural.

How to Recognize a True Sign

When you first start tuning in to the world of signs, everything can start to look like a cosmic memo. A bird lands near you? A sign! A license plate with a few repeating numbers? A sign! Your coffee tastes extra good today? Definitely a sign. While your spirit guides absolutely love sending little winks your way, it's also true that sometimes… a hummingbird is only a hummingbird. Beautiful, a little magical, but not every flutter of wings or random coincidence is meant to steer your destiny.

So how do you tell the difference? You check in with the wisest instrument you have: your body. Your body reacts to truth long before your mind finishes its little debate club routine. When something is a genuine sign for you, there's usually a noticeable shift. It can be subtle, a calmness, and a grounded feeling that says, "Yes, this is for me." For some people, it's a tingling sensation, warmth, or that gentle spark of excitement that doesn't feel frantic but feels aligned.

When it's not a sign, your body tends to stay neutral. No change. No spark. No inner "click." Simply a nice moment or a curious coincidence passing through your day without deeper resonance. Here's the trick. Don't force meaning where your body gives you nothing. Your spirit guides don't need you guessing or squinting at every cloud formation for hidden messages. They will get your attention when they need to, and your body will confirm it every time. Learning this skill is similar to building muscle memory. The more you pause, breathe, and check inward, the easier it becomes to recognize when something is truly meant for you and when it's only part of the lovely background hum of life.

A Quick Note on "False Spirit Guides" and Fear-Based Messages

Every once in a while, especially online, you'll come across warnings about "false spirit guides" or dark energies pretending to send messages. It's the spiritual equivalent of those old campfire ghost stories. Dramatic, a little spooky, and almost always exaggerated. Let me be clear: in my entire life, I have never, not even once, felt anything even close to that. I have come to realize that my spirit guides have been with me since Day One, long before I had language for them, and their presence feels as familiar and unmistakable as my mom's voice. That deep sense of safety? That warmth in your chest? That's what real guidance feels like.

But what about the "what if" that sneaks in? This is what I know. Your spirit guides don't operate through fear. Period. Their signs, nudges, and messages always hold steady, supportive energy, even when they're encouraging you toward growth or change. Still, if you ever feel uncertain or if a message feels "off," you can absolutely check. Just pause and ask, inwardly or out loud: "Are you my spirit guides who love me?" Then listen to your body again. Your instincts are wired to recognize what's true for you. If it's your real spirit guides, you'll feel clarity, warmth, ease, and that inner yes. If it's not, you'll feel nothing. Fear clouds intuition, but grounded curiosity sharpens it.

Trust what you feel. Trust the long relationship you've been building, even if you didn't always have the words for it. Your spirit guides want connection, not confusion, and they will never send you anything meant to harm or scare you.

Why Signs Sometimes Seem to Conflict

Nothing tests your sanity quite like getting two signs in the same week that point in totally opposite directions. One moment you're convinced you should go left… and the next, a feather drops out of nowhere whispering, "Actually… maybe right?" Before you assume the universe is messing with you, this is the real reason conflicting signs show up. Your question wasn't clear, your desire wasn't authentic, or the most common culprit, you unknowingly asked two different things at once.

Spirit guides are excellent at guidance, but they are

terrible at sorting through human-level wishy-washiness. If you are torn inside ("I want this… but I also want that… and please don't make me choose but also tell me what to do"), your energy sends out a mixed signal. Your spirit guides will respond, because they always respond to some degree, but their messages can end up reflecting the internal tug-of-war you haven't fully acknowledged yet.

It's not that the signs are wrong. They're just answering the version of the question you were asking in that moment. So what's the fix? You refine, you narrow, and you get specific. When your question is clean and grounded, the signs that come back will be too. They'll line up, repeat, and become unmistakable. Conflicting signs aren't your spirit guides confusing you. They're a cue that *you* need clarity first. Once you get clear inside, the outside world stops sending mixed messages.

Drilling Down to Your Real Question

When your signs seem all over the place, it's often because the question you're asking is way too big and blurry. "How do I fix my life?" is a perfect example. Your poor spirit guides are simply not sure which part of your life you are talking about. One of my favorite ways to get clarity is a simple tool sometimes called the "five whys." I learned this during my software analyst days for solving technical problems, but we're going to adapt it for spirit guide work by making it "five guided steps" so you can turn a huge, vague question into something specific that your spirit guides can actually answer. Grab a journal or notes app and try this with me.

Step 1: Start with the big, messy question. For example, let's go with: "How do I fix my life?" This is not a question your spirit guides can clearly respond to. It's more of a cry for help than a clear request. So we're going to zoom in.

Step 2: Ask yourself: "What feels most off in my life right now?" Let's say you sit with that for a moment and realize it's your job. That's where most of your dread, stress, and frustration come from.

Step 3: "Should I quit my job?" Better. Still big… but better. Your spirit guides could answer that, but you can be more specific.

Step 4: Think for a minute and try this very useful question. "If my spirit guides could help me figure out one piece of this right now, what would I most want clarity on?" Once you know, you can shape a clear, sign-friendly question.

Step 5: Turn it into a spirit guide-ready question with real specifics they can work with. Take everything you've uncovered and write a new question like: "Would leaving my current job in the next year support my long-term well-being and growth?"

Notice how your body responds. Once you have a clear question, pause. Say it out loud. You will feel a sense of relief, like that's what you really wanted to know. That's your inner confirmation that you've drilled down far enough. From here, this is the question you bring to your spirit guides. This is what you ask for signs about, and because you've cleared away the vague, tangled "fix my whole life" energy, the signs you get are much more likely to align, repeat, and actually make sense.

You can use this same process with anything: relationships, money, moving, creative dreams, and beyond. Any time your signs feel conflicted, come back to this drill-down process. Clear question in, clear guidance out.

What If I Make a Mistake and Get the Sign Wrong?

This is a classic worry. The "What if I misread the sign and accidentally ruin my life?" spiral. You are not alone. Everyone hits this fear at some point. I know I do, especially when signs start showing up more often, and it suddenly feels as if choosing a cereal brand could alter the course of destiny. Luckily, you are allowed to interpret a sign imperfectly. You are allowed to make a guess, try something, course-correct, and learn. Your spirit guides are not standing in the corner with a red marker grading your performance. They're walking with you, nudging you, encouraging you, and redirecting you when needed.

Think of it as turning on your GPS. If you miss a turn, it doesn't scream, "Well, that's it. Good luck in the wilderness." It simply recalculates and gently points you toward the next best step. Your spirit guides work exactly the same way. What brings the most relief is if you truly misread a sign, you will know. Your body will tell you. The energy will feel off. Things won't click the way real alignment does. When that happens, your spirit guides will send a new sign, a clearer one, to help steer you back.

You cannot get this "wrong" in a way that derails your true life's purpose. You're not being tested. You're being supported. The whole point of signs is connection, not pressure. So, check in with your body, and remember that your spirit guides know exactly how to reach you, even when you take a detour.

When the Signs Go Silent

There will be moments, sometimes days, maybe even a

stretch of weeks, when the signs seem to dry up like someone accidentally unplugged the coffee maker. No feathers. No numbers. No nudges. Nothing obvious is happening. It can feel unsettling, especially once you've gotten used to guidance showing up regularly. You might start wondering if you did something wrong, or if your spirit guides got busy helping someone else (never going to happen), or if the connection somehow disappeared. Take a breath. This silence is not abandonment and it's not punishment. It's a pause and pauses have purpose. Here are a few reasons the signs may go quiet.

1. You already have the guidance you need. Sometimes your spirit guides step back because they've given you the message, you've acknowledged you got it, and now it's your turn to act, integrate, or simply live it out. Silence here is confidence in you, not distance.

2. You're in a growth moment that requires your own voice. Think of it as similar to learning to ride a bike. At some point, the steadying hand lifts. Not because you're alone, but because you're ready to feel your own balance.

3. You're energetically overwhelmed. Big life transitions, stress, grief, or emotional overload can create "static." Signs may still be coming, but you're too full to register them. Once you ground yourself and breathe again, the messages start flowing more easily.

No matter the reason, remember this. Silence does not mean disconnection. Your spirit guides don't wander off or forget you exist. They stay right where they always are, steady, loving, and patient, waiting for the right moment to reach you again. If you want to reconnect, try something simple. Put a hand on your heart or stomach, take a quiet breath, and say, "I'm here. Whenever you're ready, I'm listening." Trust that when the silence ends, and it always does, the signs will return clearer and stronger than before.

Building Confidence in Your Interpretation

Confidence doesn't usually arrive in one big lightning bolt. It's a slow and steady process. When you're learning to follow your signs and trust your spirit guides, you're really learning to trust yourself. That takes practice, patience, and a little willingness to wobble. Think about it. Every new skill in life begins with uncertainty. The first time you tried to drive, cook, meditate, or even text with your thumbs, you were clumsy. You hesitated. You second-guessed every move, but it didn't stay that way, and you got better because you kept showing up. Interpreting signs works exactly the same way.

The biggest misconception is that people who trust their signs do so because they're fearless. That's not true. They simply allow themselves to follow the tiny nudges, make educated guesses, and learn from what unfolds. They know mistakes aren't really mistakes, they're clarifying moments, and clarity is confidence's best friend. One of the easiest ways to strengthen that confidence is to look back at times you already recognized guidance without realizing it. Think about moments when you said yes to something that changed your life in a good way, even though logic said no. Or times when you walked away from a bad situation that felt wrong before you could explain why. Those weren't random. That was your inner knowing partnering with your spirit guides long before you consciously invited them in. The more you acknowledge those moments, the more you realize you've been doing this for years. That recognition alone builds solid trust.

Another key piece is learning to honor the signals your body gives you. The sensations of alignment, softness, groundedness, and a little expanding warmth are incredibly reliable. When something is meant for you, your whole being relaxes. When something isn't, you tighten, hesitate, or feel foggy. Your body is the tuning fork for truth. The more you listen, the clearer it rings. Remember, you can practice checking in with your spirit guides in low-stakes moments. Ask for a sign about something simple, like which walk to take or which book to pick up next. As you follow through and notice the results, your confidence doesn't only grow, it compounds. Soon, you're no longer hopeful that something is right. You *know* what feels right and you trust it. Your spirit guides don't need perfection from you. They simply need openness.

As you grow more confident in recognizing and following signs, you may notice a desire to support that process in simple, tangible ways. Not because your intuition needs help, but because having something to anchor your attention can make the connection feel steadier and more intentional. Signs teach you how guidance moves through the world, while tools simply give you a place to meet it. In the next chapter, we'll explore a few optional tools that can deepen your connection with your spirit guides and help you tune in with a little more focus, comfort, and ease.

15

Tools That Deepen Your Connection

You don't need any special tools to work with your spirit guides (I know I've mentioned that many times). Truly. They don't sit around wringing their hands, hoping you'll finally buy a rose-quartz tower the size of a houseplant. They don't require a candle, a tarot deck, or a single shiny object from the metaphysical store. But… if you want to use them? Your spirit guides will absolutely light up as if you invited them to a surprise party in their honor.

Think of these tools as atmospheric enhancers. They don't create the connection. You already did that. They can, however, simply give your mind, your energy, and your intention a place to gather. Sometimes that little gathering spot, that tiny ceremony of "I'm here, I'm listening," helps everything flow more easily. Let's walk through a few of the most common tools people reach for when they want to feel a smidge more plugged in.

Crystals: Nature's Pocket Helpers

Crystals are tiny companions you can slip into a

pocket, set on your desk, or hold in your hand when you want a little extra sense of grounding. They're not required equipment for connecting with your spirit guides, but they can be lovely little helpers that make the whole experience feel more intentional. Think of them as the cozy throw blanket of spiritual tools. Absolutely not necessary, but delightful if you enjoy them.

Some people feel a gentle energy when they hold certain stones. Others simply enjoy the weight, the temperature, or the beauty of them. Plenty of people appreciate the symbolism. One type of stone means clarity, another stone means peace, or reminds me to stay open. All those reasons are perfectly valid. You don't have to believe in anything special for crystals to support your mindset.

Spirit guides love when you use anything that helps you show up more fully. When you pick up a crystal, you're essentially pausing and opening yourself to purposefully listen. That moment of focus is what delights them, not the mineral structure of quartz. Crystals help you shift into a clearer internal space. They give your hands something to do while your intuition warms up. They anchor you in your body, so your mind doesn't go wandering into grocery lists and errands. They create a tiny ceremonial feeling. Just enough to signal that this isn't ordinary time. This is connection time.

Pick one stone (I include a short list of some of my favorites later in the book) or pick none. You're not earning gold stars here. Your spirit guides aren't scoring your collection. They simply appreciate anything that helps your energy focus and your attention settle. If you do decide to bring crystals into your practice, let them be simple. Let them be intuitive. Let them be fun. Spirit guides adore when you add elements that make the connection feel pleasurable and inviting because the more you enjoy the process, the more often you'll show up.

Candles: Setting the Mood (Literally)

A single candle can shift the entire feel of a moment. There's something about a soft flame that naturally quiets the mind. It reminds you to take a breath and settle in. That stillness is what makes candles such a gentle tool for connecting with your spirit guides. You're not summoning anything mystical. You're simply creating an atmosphere where your attention can focus more easily. Lighting a candle before you check in with your spirit guides is a bit like dimming the lights before a favorite movie. It doesn't change the story, but it absolutely enhances your experience of it. The flame becomes a steady point for your eyes, your breath, and your intention to gather around. And your spirit guides? They love it when you create these little pockets of presence. It's as if you're rolling out a soft welcome mat. The best part? Candles don't require any ceremony beyond your comfort level. You can go full ambiance with scents, colors, or beautiful holders, or you can grab the nearest tea light and call it good. The type of candle doesn't matter. The color doesn't matter (although I talk about that later in the book, too). You don't need to memorize correspondences like you're studying for a magical final exam. What matters is the moment you create.

When you strike a match, you're sending a subtle signal to yourself that you are shifting gears now and tuning in. That's the moment your energy changes and your spirit guides feel that shift instantly. If you enjoy scents, choose one that makes you feel open or calm. Lavender for stillness. Vanilla for comfort. Citrus when you need a little lift.

Or skip scent altogether if you want something simple and clean. Some people light candles when they journal to their spirit guides, others when they meditate, and others simply when they need a moment of steadying before asking a question.

Candles also work beautifully when guidance feels distant or static. Not because the flame magically "calls" your spirit guides, but because it helps you come back into your body, into your breath, into right-now and clarity loves "right-now." Use candles if they help you feel present. Use them if they make the moment feel intentional. Use them if they bring you comfort or a sense of ritual that feels cozy instead of complicated. But if candles aren't your thing? Your spirit guides won't mind one bit.

A Simple Altar: Your Connection Corner

Let's take a deep breath and soften this word right out of the gate: altar. For a lot of people, that word comes with old baggage, whether it's religious, mystical, dramatic, or intimidating. But in the context of spirit guide connection, an altar is simply a spot where your intention lives. Nothing more. Nothing spooky. Nothing ceremonial unless you choose it to be. Here's the biggest truth. You absolutely do not need an altar to connect with your spirit guides. Many people go their whole lives connecting with their spirit guides beautifully without ever having one. So if the idea makes you nervous, curious, or even a little resistant (or, heaven forbid, close this book), that's okay. This is an invitation, not a requirement.

Altars can be tiny. I mean truly tiny. A corner of a shelf. A top of a dresser. A windowsill. Even a single object placed somewhere meaningful to you. They can also be larger if that feels good to you, but bigger isn't better. This isn't about size. It's about intention. When I first started, mine was in my closet. Yup. Literally the closet. I was afraid someone would see it and think I'd gone off the mystical deep end. Yet, that tiny, hidden corner became the first place where I allowed myself to show up fully with my spirit guides. Over time, as I grew more confident and comfortable, that little private nook transformed. Now? My altar sits proudly in my office, out in the open, because connection has become something I'm no longer shy about. Hey, I even write books about it.

If you want to create your own, here's the simplest place to start. Choose a spot that feels calm or inviting. Then place one or two things there that help you shift into a clearer state when you see them. That's it. Zero drama. Some easy, judgment-free ideas are a candle you light when you want to tune in or a crystal or stone that feels grounding. Add a feather you found on a walk or a photograph that inspires you. It can be a small bowl for tiny meaningful objects or a sticky note with a word like "listen," "trust," or "open." If you want color, consider white, blue, or gold because all are gentle, connective tones, but again, you call the shots.

What do you use an altar for? Anything that helps you shift into the mindset of connection. It can be a place to take one slow breath before asking your spirit guides a question, a spot to journal or pull an oracle card, or simply somewhere to say "hello" or "thank you." Mostly, it's a quiet corner for reflection or clarity and serves as a touchpoint throughout your day that reminds you your spirit guides are close. If it helps, think of an altar as a landing pad. Not a magical one, but a psychological one. It's a place your energy recognizes as where you show up differently. Your spirit guides adore that. Not because they need props, but because they love when you create space where you're more receptive, intentional, and open.

Still, if you never build an altar, you'll continue to connect beautifully. But if you do? It can become a comforting little anchor. A spot you return to again and again, not because you're obligated, but because you want to.

Try This Little Moment of Connection

Here's something simple you can experiment with, to see how it feels. Nothing formal, and nothing elaborate, but more like a tiny invitation to slow down and tune in.

Choose one item you feel drawn to today. It could be a crystal you already have, or a candle you light for a bit of atmosphere, or a small spot you've unofficially decided is your "connection corner." If you're curious, choose two. Or all three. There are no rules here. Once you've picked your items, give yourself a quiet minute to settle in. Sit comfortably. Take a slow breath. Let your body relax. Now, bring your attention to your chosen objects.

Hold the crystal if you picked one. Light the candle and watch the flame for a few seconds. If you're sitting near your little altar spot, let it become your focal point. Now, say a greeting in your mind or out loud. A simple "hello" and "I'm here" works. That's enough. Your spirit guides instantly feel the shift when you turn your attention toward them. Notice what changes. Do your thoughts feel clearer or more settled? Does the answer to a question you've been thinking about come to you? Maybe nothing shifts at all, and that's completely normal, too. You're only experimenting.

Stay for one or two more breaths, then go on with your day. No pressure to receive a message. No pressure to feel anything special. This is simply you exploring what supports your clarity and connection. Try this again tomorrow or next week with a different combination. Maybe a candle only, a crystal only, both together or at your altar space. You may discover that one setup feels surprisingly supportive… or that you prefer keeping things simple and doing none of these. Regardless, your spirit guides are delighted whenever you show up with even a whisper of intention.

How These Tools Support (Not Replace) Your Inner Connection

At the heart of everything in this book and everything in your relationship with your spirit guides is this truth: the connection lives inside you. It is not in a crystal or in a candle flame. It is not on an altar. Those things can deepen the experience, but they will never be the source of it. You are the source. Your awareness, your willingness, and your curiosity are the living bridge between you and your spirit guides.

These tools simply help you settle into that bridge more fully. They create atmosphere, intention, and a shift in mindset. Lighting a candle signals you are present. Holding a crystal helps your body calm enough to listen. Sitting at your altar becomes a cue that you're stepping into a moment of listening. Each of these tools is like turning down the volume on the outer world so you can hear the inner one more clearly. But they don't do the connecting for you, and they never will. Your spirit guides don't measure your devotion by the size of your altar or the price of your stones. They aren't impressed by elaborate rituals or discouraged by simple ones. They care about your openness, your honesty, and your desire to show up. Whether you greet them with nothing but your breath or you light a dozen candles, the connection is the same. Your intention is what they respond to.

So use these tools if they make the moment feel richer, calmer, or more meaningful. Let them support you, anchor you, or give you something to look forward to. And if you prefer a minimalist approach? Beautiful. Your spirit guides love that too. There is no wrong way to connect when the connection comes from within. However you choose to show up, whether it's quiet, casual, elaborate, or somewhere in between, your spirit guides are already there, meeting you every time.

As you explore which tools feel supportive to you, you may notice that some elements speak louder than others. Color, light, and atmosphere often reach us before words do, shifting our energy in quiet but powerful ways. These subtle cues are another language your spirit guides love to use, one that works directly with your senses and emotions. In the following few chapters, we'll dive deeper into how colors, candles, crystals, and altars can deepen your connection and help guidance come through with greater clarity, warmth, and ease.

16

Colors & Candles & Light

There's a reason humans have always reached for color and light when seeking something beyond ourselves. Long before any of us knew the words "spirit guides," we instinctively lit candles for comfort, wrapped ourselves in certain colors when we needed courage, or felt strangely soothed by the soft glow of a flame. These things aren't magic on their own, but they do help us tune our energy, quiet the noise, and open the door a little wider to guidance that's already trying to reach us.

Think of colors and candles as helpers, not requirements. You don't need a shelf full of fancy supplies or an altar that looks as if it belongs in a museum. Even a single candle you light with intention, or a color you choose because it feels right, can shift your awareness just enough to catch a message you might have missed. Your spirit guides love working through simple tools like these because they help you slow down, focus, and feel more connected to the conversation that's already happening. As you explore these colors, pay attention to the ones that tug at you, comfort you, or energize you. That feeling is part of the guidance too.

Blue — Communication & Calm Insight

Blue is the color your spirit guides reach for when they want to get a message through without drama or static. When blue shows up as a sign (such as a blue feather), it means they are near and listening. It is their way of nudging you into clarity and reminding you that you're not guessing… you're receiving.

Using blue intentionally helps open the channels even further. Lighting a blue candle is similar to sending an invitation: "I'm ready to hear you." The flame softens mental noise and supports calm, intuitive communication. Placing something blue on your altar turns the space into a gentle beacon for guidance. It signals that you're open, grounded, and willing to receive insight with honesty and courage. Blue is the steady voice of your spirit guides. When in doubt, start there.

White — Clarity & Pure Connection

White is the color of clean channels and fresh starts. When it appears as a sign, your spirit guides are often telling you that the answer you are seeking is simpler than you think. White sweeps away mental clutter and helps you see the truth beneath all the overthinking.

Using white intentionally deepens your connection. Lighting a white candle creates a kind of spiritual blank slate, making it easier for your spirit guides to communicate without interference from doubt or emotional static. It's especially powerful when you're asking for direction on something tangled or overwhelming. A white object on your altar, such as a stone, a shell, or even a simple tea light, acts as a focus point for clean guidance and protection.

Purple — Wisdom, Intuition & Higher-Realm Connection

Purple is the color of deep spiritual knowing. The kind that doesn't come from logic but from that clear inner "click" when truth finally reveals itself. When purple shows up as a sign, your spirit guides are telling you to trust what you already know. Your intuition is leading you well. Purple signals a shift into higher awareness and insight.

Using purple intentionally helps lift your connection to a higher, more intuitive frequency. Lighting a purple candle can turn your space into a quiet doorway to the spiritual realm, making it easier to understand subtle messages or see patterns you've been missing. Adding something purple to your altar acts as a reminder that wisdom isn't out there somewhere—it's rising from within you. Purple shows up when your spirit guides want to take the conversation deeper and when you're ready for the next level of understanding.

Pink — Love, Support & Heart-Led Guidance

Pink is the color your spirit guides use when they want to speak directly to your heart. When pink shows up as a sign, it is the spirit guides telling you to breathe and know you're loved and safe. Pink carries reassurance, emotional healing, and the reminder that guidance doesn't always arrive as a directive. Sometimes it arrives as comfort.

Using pink intentionally helps open your heart to receive messages without fear or self-doubt getting in the way. A pink candle invites gentle, compassionate communication and is perfect for moments when you're anxious, grieving, or need a little extra emotional grounding. Placing something pink on your altar calls in kindness and softens whatever you've been bracing behind. Pink shows up when your spirit guides want you to feel supported, not overwhelmed. It whispers, "You don't have to do this alone."

Red — Courage, Action & Empowered Guidance

Red is the color of movement. It appears the moment your spirit guides step in and tells you that you are stronger than you think. When red shows up as a sign, it's often a nudge toward courage or a reminder that your next step is ready for you. Red signals momentum, confidence, and the inner fire needed to take action.

Using red intentionally helps call in that bold, supportive energy. Lighting a red candle can strengthen your resolve, especially when you're facing a crossroads or trying to shake off fear-based hesitation. It's the "I'm ready to step forward" color. Adding something red to your altar invites your spirit guides to back you with bravery and a clear sense of direction. Red arrives when your spirit guides want to remind you that you are not fragile. You are powerful, capable, and ready to move.

Orange — Creativity, Confidence & Inspired Action

Orange is the color your spirit guides use when they're trying to light you up from the inside out. When it appears as a sign, it often means it is time to follow the spark because something exciting is trying to be born. Orange brings confidence, joy, and that delicious sense of possibility that gets ideas moving again.

Using orange intentionally helps stir inspiration and clear away hesitation. Lighting an orange candle is wonderful when you want guidance that energizes and inspires you (for example, I burn an orange candle while I write this because I'm bringing words and ideas into the world). Adding something orange to your altar invites playful and creative communication from your spirit guides. It's especially helpful when you're starting new projects or trying to reconnect with your natural enthusiasm. Orange shows up when your spirit guides want to remind you that intuition can be fun and that the path forward doesn't have to feel heavy.

Yellow — Insight, Optimism & Mental Clarity

Yellow is the color of those "aha" moments your spirit guides love to deliver. When yellow shows up as a sign, it often means you need to pay attention because the answer is trying to reach you. Yellow brings mental brightness, hope, and the kind of clear perspective that cuts through confusion.

Using yellow intentionally helps open your mind to guidance that is direct, practical, and illuminating. Lighting a yellow candle invites insight and is perfect for moments when you want clarity on a situation or need help seeing the bigger picture. Adding something yellow to your altar acts as a beacon for positive, clarifying messages. Yellow shows up when your spirit guides want to brighten your thinking and remind you that solutions are within reach, often closer than you realize.

Green — Healing, Prosperity & Compassionate Growth

Green is the color your spirit guides send when something in your life is ready to flourish, whether it be emotionally, spiritually, or even materially. When green appears as a sign, it often means that growth is available and it's time to trust the process. Green holds the energy of healing, renewal, and prosperity. Not only financial abundance, but a richer, more supported life overall.

Using green intentionally invites guidance that strengthens both your heart and your stability. Lighting a green candle encourages grounded insight around healing, relationships, and opportunities for abundance. Adding something green to your altar calls in steady, earth-based support that helps your intentions take root and thrive. Green shows up when your spirit guides want you to know that growth is happening on multiple levels and that expansion, in every sense, is on its way.

Black — Protection, Boundaries & Deep Inner Truth

Black is often misunderstood, but your spirit guides use it in the most loving way. When black shows up as a sign, it means your spirit guides are protecting you and it is okay to step forward. Black invites you to explore your inner world with courage rather than fear. It's the color of honest reflection, shadow healing, and strong energetic boundaries.

Using black intentionally creates a safe container for guidance. Lighting a black candle helps absorb energetic noise and sets a clear, firm boundary between you and whatever isn't yours to carry. It's especially powerful when you feel overwhelmed, drained, or unsure what emotions actually belong to you. Adding something black to your altar anchors your space with protection and grounding. Black shows up when your spirit guides want you to feel safe enough to go deeper, knowing you're held every step of the way.

Gold — Divine Support, Abundance & Confident Alignment

Gold is the color of guidance that comes with that unmistakable feeling of being on exactly the right path. When gold appears as a sign, your spirit guides are signaling that everything is aligned. Gold carries divine encouragement, abundance, and the inner confidence that blooms when everything starts clicking into place.

Using gold intentionally invites high-vibration support and a sense of purpose. Lighting a gold or gold-toned candle helps strengthen your connection to guidance that is uplifting, expansive, and deeply affirming. Adding something gold to your altar amplifies abundance energy and reminds you that your spirit guides are helping weave opportunities behind the scenes. Gold shows up when your spirit guides want you to stand tall, trust your direction, and receive the blessings that are already moving toward you.

Silver — Intuition, Dreams & Gentle Guidance

Silver is the color your spirit guides use when they want to slip a message into your awareness softly through dreams, synchronicities, or intuitive nudges that feel almost whispered. When silver appears as a sign, it often means it is time to slow down and listen. Something subtle but important is coming through. Silver carries inner wisdom and the quiet kind of insight that reveals itself when you're still.

Using silver intentionally strengthens your connection with intuitive and dream-based guidance. Lighting a silver candle during moon phases (especially the full or new moon) helps open channels for messages that arrive through symbols and feelings rather than words. Adding something silver to your altar invites your spirit guides to speak to you in the gentlest, most intuitive ways. Silver shows up when your spirit guides want to fine-tune your senses so you can catch the delicate signs you might otherwise miss.

Colors and candles aren't about creating a perfect ritual. They're about creating a moment. A pause in your day where you breathe, settle your energy, and let your spirit guides step a little closer. These tools don't replace your intuition. They strengthen it. They help you recognize your own inner signals more clearly, and remind you that guidance can be simple, gentle, and woven into everyday life.

As you experiment, notice what feels natural. Notice which colors seem to follow you around, which candles you reach for without thinking, and which moments feel a little brighter or more aligned after you light a flame. Your spirit guides will meet you wherever you are, whether you light a candle once a week or simply become more aware of the colors appearing in your path. Use what resonates, ignore what doesn't, and let this be an easy relationship rather than a chore. Your spirit guides aren't grading your technique. They're celebrating every small step you take toward connection. And remember that every time you pause, breathe, and open the door, even a crack, they cheerfully walk through.

17

Crystals That Turn Up the Volume on Spirit Messages

Connecting with your spirit guides doesn't require owning a museum-grade crystal collection, but let's be honest, a few shiny companions never hurt anyone. (Trust me, I have a lot of them). Crystals have been used for centuries as little energy anchors and tools that help us focus our intention, settle our mind, and create an atmosphere where guidance can be felt more easily. Think of them as supportive sidekicks, not superheroes. They don't do the work for you, but they absolutely help you tune in, calm down, and stay open.

Some crystals feel like warm hugs. Others feel like flipping a light switch. A few might feel like nothing at all until suddenly, during a meditation or a moment of doubt, you realize you're holding exactly the right stone at exactly the right time. That's the beauty of working with crystals. They nudge your inner senses awake in ways that are gentle, grounding, and sometimes downright magical.

Amethyst — The Intuition Whisperer

If crystals had job titles, the amethyst would be the Director of Spiritual Communication. Its deep violet color has long been associated with intuition, clearness, and the higher mind. Basically, the exact qualities you want switched on when you're hoping to connect with your spirit guides. That purple hue isn't only pretty. It carries the energetic vibration where intuition wakes up, expands, and begins sending you more moments of clarity.

Amethyst works because it calms the noise. When your thoughts are bouncing everywhere, your spirit guides can be waving their arms like air-traffic controllers, and you still don't notice. Amethyst helps quiet that inner storm. It settles the nervous system, slows your thoughts, and opens the energetic doorway so guidance can slip through without fighting for your attention.

You can use amethyst in meditation, keep it on your nightstand for dream guidance, place it by your workspace for clearer intuitive nudges, or hold it when you're asking your spirit guides a question. Its energy is steady, supportive, and non-dramatic, kind of like the friend who always picks up your call, listens without judgment, and gently tells you exactly what you needed to hear.

Clear Quartz — The Amplifier

If amethyst is the intuitive whisperer, clear quartz is the megaphone. This crystal is all about focus and turning up the volume on whatever intention you're working with. Its transparent, shimmering appearance says nothing is hidden, nothing is complicated, just clean, bright energy that helps you see and feel things more clearly. Clear quartz works by amplifying your intuition, your signals to your spirit guides, your sense of direction, and even your ability to stay present. Think of it as a booster that strengthens the connection you already have. If you're trying to tune in to your spirit guides and feel like the signal keeps cutting out, clear quartz helps sharpen the frequency so you're not guessing in the dark.

It's also wonderfully versatile. You can pair it with any other crystal to enhance its effect, hold it while journaling your questions to your spirit guides, keep it near your workspace to stay mentally sharp, or use it during meditation to help your mind settle faster. Clear quartz doesn't try to take over. It simply supports whatever you're already doing, giving your inner guidance system a brighter, cleaner channel to work through.

Rose Quartz — The Heart Opener

Rose quartz may be soft pink, but make no mistake, it's powerful. This is the stone of compassion, emotional calm, and that gentle feeling of being held by something loving. That matters more than people realize, because spirit guides communicate best when your heart feels safe and open, not guarded or bracing for impact. The rose quartz carries the energy of comfort and reassurance. It helps soften self-doubt, dissolve tension, and create a warm internal space where guidance can settle. When your heart is tight or your emotions feel prickly, messages from your spirit guides can get lost in the noise. Rose quartz relaxes that tightness. It reminds you that you're loved, supported, and not going through any of this alone.

Use rose quartz when you're feeling overwhelmed, insecure, or disconnected from your sense of worth. Keep it on your nightstand to soothe your dreams (I have some on a shelf above my headboard), hold it during meditation to soften your emotional edges, or place it somewhere you'll see often as a quiet reminder to be kind to yourself. Rose quartz doesn't only help you receive guidance. It helps you believe you're worthy of receiving it in the first place.

Labradorite — The Magic Mirror

If there's a crystal that practically shouts "mystic energy," it's labradorite. With its flashes of blue, gold, and green shimmering beneath a smoky surface, this stone has long been associated with intuition, transformation, and seeing beyond the obvious. In other words, it helps you spot the subtle nudges and quiet signs your spirit guides slip into your day. What makes labradorite work so beautifully is its reflective quality. Those shifting colors mimic the way intuition often appears. Not as a big neon sign, but as a flicker of insight, a sudden knowing, or a feeling you can't quite explain. Labradorite helps you notice those flickers instead of brushing them off as "random." It strengthens your ability to catch the signs you might normally overlook.

This stone is especially great when your spirit guides are sending synchronicities, symbols, or gut feelings and you want to sharpen your awareness. Keep it nearby while journaling about signs, hold it before meditation to open your inner senses, or carry it on days when you want to stay extra tuned in.

Lapis Lazuli — The Truth Teller

Lapis Lazuli, or simply lapis, is the stone that looks as if it was carved from a twilight sky, with its deep blue and little sparkles. Historically, it's been linked with wisdom, insight, and speaking truth, which makes it a fantastic partner when you're trying to understand and articulate the guidance your spirit guides are sending (it is not by accident that I wear a lapis lazuli and silver ring on my right hand). Lapis works because it brings your inner and outer worlds into alignment. It helps you trust those intuitive hits, those sudden realizations, and gives you the confidence to put them into words. When your spirit guides send you a nudge, lapis helps you interpret it without second-guessing yourself into oblivion.

Keep lapis close when you're journaling questions for your spirit guides, having important conversations, or trying to get clear about what you really feel. It supports honest self-reflection and helps you express your intuitive insights with clarity and confidence.

Blue Kyanite — The Align-Without-Trying Stone

Blue kyanite has a sleek, blade-like look that gives away its superpower: cutting through the energetic clutter that blocks guidance. Its energy is crisp, clean, and incredibly stabilizing, helping you stay centered even when life feels like a three-ring circus. Kyanite works by bringing your thoughts, emotions, and inner senses into harmony so your connection with your spirit guides isn't constantly getting jammed. When your mind is scattered or you feel energetically "tilted," kyanite helps you stabilize without forcing anything. It's gentle but direct, similar to someone putting a steady hand on your back and reminding you that you're okay.

Use blue kyanite when you want clarity, balance, and a smooth, uninterrupted intuitive flow. It's wonderful during meditation, during any kind of spiritual journaling, or simply carried with you on days when you need mental steadiness and emotional neutrality.

Fluorite — The Focus Finder

Fluorite looks like a crystal that wandered out of a watercolor painting with bands of green, purple, and blue. Its calm, layered colors reflect what it does best, which is bringing order to chaos. When your mind feels similar to a busy intersection and your spirit guides are trying to get a message through, fluorite steps in as the friendly traffic cop. This stone helps filter out distractions, both internal and external, so you can home in on the intuitive nudges that actually matter. It improves focus, sharpens mental clarity, and gently quiets the noise of overthinking. If you've ever wished your intuition came with a highlighter, fluorite is that highlighter.

Keep fluorite on your desk (I have it on mine!), hold it before meditation, or use it when you're analyzing signs and trying to understand what your spirit guides are really saying. Its energy is grounding without being heavy, and clarifying without being stern.

Moonstone — The Inner Tide-Turner

Moonstone glows with that soft, pearly shimmer that makes you feel as if you're holding a sliver of moonlight. It's long been associated with intuition, emotional flow, and that quiet inner knowing that often whispers long before your logical mind catches up. If you've ever felt guidance arrive as a nudge rather than a declaration, moonstone helps you hear those nudges more clearly. This stone works by softening emotional resistance. When you're too tense, guarded, or overthinking the signs your spirit guides send, moonstone calms the waters. It helps you stay open, receptive, and aware of the subtle shifts happening inside you. That's where ninety-nine percent of intuitive information shows up first, not in your thoughts, but in your feelings.

Moonstone is especially wonderful for dream work, reflective journaling, and those days when you want to understand your inner tides a little better. Place it on your nightstand, meditate with it when you're feeling unsure, or carry it when you want to stay emotionally attuned to your spirit guides' messages.

Black Tourmaline — The Grounding Guardrail

At first glance, black tourmaline doesn't look flashy. No sparkle, no shimmer, but also no drama. Still, don't let the simplicity fool you. This is one of the strongest protective stones out there, and a powerful ally for anyone building a relationship with their spirit guides. Its job is simple. It is to keep your energetic space clean so your intuition doesn't have to fight through static. Black tourmaline works by grounding and stabilizing your energy. When you're anxious, overwhelmed, or emotionally scattered, intuitive messages can feel faint or inconsistent. Black tourmaline drops an anchor. It helps release the noise, tension, and "what if" energy that muddies the water and makes it harder to trust what you're sensing.

Keep this stone near your front door, by your workspace, or close during meditation. Keep it anywhere you want a sense of stability and protection (it works great and looks beautiful as a bracelet). It creates the kind of steady inner foundation where spirit guide connection thrives.

Crystals are wonderful companions on the path of spiritual connection, but remember, they're support tools, not requirements. You don't need a giant collection of rare stones mined under a full moon by ancient monks. You only need one or two that feel good in your hand or pocket and help you shift into the energy of openness, curiosity, and calm awareness. Use these stones to quiet your mind, ground your body, soften your heart, or focus your attention. Let them be touchstones, little reminders that your spirit guides are always ready to connect, and that you're learning how to listen more clearly every day. The magic isn't in the crystal. The magic is in you. The stone just helps you tune the channel a little faster.

18

Tarot Cards as a Conversation

Tarot cards get a reputation for being a little woo, and honestly? Fair enough. You're shuffling illustrated cards and asking the universe to speak through pictures. It sounds odd until you try it and then, suddenly, it's not odd at all. It's clarifying. It's grounding. It's surprisingly direct. When it comes to communicating with your spirit guides, tarot cards can become a wonderful translator between their world and yours. Now, let me be clear: you absolutely do not need tarot cards to connect with your spirit guides. They'll talk to you through signs, nudges, synchronicities, and gut feelings. Tarot cards are simply one more tool you can use if they appeal to you. Think of it as a conversation starter. Your spirit guides already know how to communicate with you. Tarot cards simply give them another, often clearer, channel to send a message through.

For this book, we're only working with the Major Arcana, the twenty-two cards that represent the big themes of the human spiritual journey. They cut right to the chase. They don't sweat the small stuff. They speak to the soul-level message your spirit guides want you to hear. Events, fears, hopes, awakenings, endings, beginnings… the Major Arcana covers the entire arc of transformation. That's why we use them here. They keep the conversation simple and powerful.

The descriptions that follow come from the traditional Rider-Waite Smith deck. This is the one you've probably seen in movies or on a bookshelf at some point. Most decks follow a similar structure, even if the artwork and mood are wildly different. One of my personal favorites is the Cat Tarot deck (it's smiling at me right here on my desk). It's playful, lighthearted, and absolutely not scary. And believe me, your spirit guides don't mind a little humor. In fact, I believe they love it, but most importantly, they meet you where you are, even if where you are happens to be a deck full of mischievous felines.

Tarot decks are easy to find. Metaphysical shops almost always carry them, but so do plenty of regular bookstores and basically every online retailer. There's no complicated ritual required to pull a card. No moonlight cleansing, chanting, or special velvet cloth (unless you want one, in which case go wild). To use tarot cards as a conversation with your spirit guides, simply take the twenty-two Major Arcana cards out of a regular deck, give them a good shuffle, and draw one card… or three… or however many you feel nudged to pull. The point here isn't perfection. It's openness. Shuffle, draw, take a breath, and interpret the message. Your spirit guides are already whispering to you. The tarot cards simply help you hear them a little more clearly.

0 The Fool – New beginnings, Trusting the Nudge, and Taking First Steps

This card is a spark of pure possibility. The Fool is the

soul at the edge of a new beginning, open-hearted, curious, and willing to trust the journey even without knowing the whole map. It's the moment before the first step when anything is still possible. When you pull it from the deck, your spirit guides are nudging you to say yes. Yes to the unknown. Yes to the nudge you keep feeling. Yes to the path that doesn't make total sense yet but feels right. They're reminding you that innocence isn't naivety. It's openness and openness lets things happen.

The best way to use this message is to take one small step toward the thing that's been whispering in your ear. You don't have to see the entire staircase, only the next foothold. Ask your spirit guides to walk with you, stay curious, and allow the next breadcrumb to appear. Trust that you're supported, even if the path hasn't fully formed yet.

I The Magician – Personal Power, Focused Intention, and Turning Ideas into Action

This card is the embodiment of personal power. The Magician stands between heaven and earth, reminding you that you already hold everything you need to create what you desire. When you pull this card, your spirit guides want you to see that the idea, talent, or calling stirring within you is ready to be brought to life through your intention and action.

The best way to use this message is to choose one thing you want to manifest and take a clear, deliberate step toward it today. Focus your energy like a beam instead of scattering it in every direction. Write it, say it, plan it, or best of all, start it. Anything that makes it real. Your spirit guides will meet you the moment you commit, amplifying your efforts and helping the path unfold.

II The High Priestess – Intuition, Inner Knowing, and Quiet Spiritual Wisdom

This card is the keeper of intuition, inner knowing, and the mysteries that can't be explained with logic alone. The High Priestess sits between the seen and unseen worlds, inviting you to slow down, listen, and trust what rises from within. When she appears, your spirit guides are encouraging you to honor your instincts, your dreams, your gut feelings, and the quiet truths you've been sensing but maybe second-guessing.

The best way to use this message is to create space for stillness and pay attention to whatever bubbles up. Pause before taking action. Journal the first thing that comes to mind. Notice patterns in your dreams. Let your spirit guides speak through subtlety instead of seeking loud, obvious signs. The High Priestess reminds you that your intuition is a sacred doorway and it opens when you trust your inner voice long before you need anyone else to validate it.

III The Empress – Nurturing Energy, Creativity, and Abundance

This card is pure abundance, creativity, and the soft, steady warmth of being supported by your spirit guides. The Empress embodies growth in all forms: ideas, relationships, healing, and even the simple pleasure of feeling at home in your own skin. When she shows up, your spirit guides are reminding you that you deserve to receive as much as you give. They're nudging you toward comfort, beauty, and self-care, but also toward trusting that something you've been thinking about is ready to flourish.

The best way to use this message is to lean into nourishment. Do one thing that feeds your body, your creativity, or your emotional well-being. Give attention to the thing that's growing in your life right now and treat it gently, like a seed that knows exactly how to become a tree. Your spirit guides want you to relax into receiving, to stop forcing outcomes, and to let expansion happen naturally. The Empress reminds you that when you care for yourself, everything else grows with ease.

IV The Emperor – Structure, Stability, and Confident Leadership

This card is the embodiment of structure, stability, and grounded leadership. The Emperor represents boundaries, authority, and the kind of steady presence that brings order to chaos. When he appears, your spirit guides are encouraging you to step into your power, not with force, but with clarity. This is a reminder that discipline doesn't limit you. It frees you to build the life you want.

The best way to use this message is to decide where you need a little more structure or where you've been letting uncertainty take the wheel. Set one firm boundary. Make one clear plan. Take ownership of something instead of waiting for someone else to lead. Your spirit guides want you to trust your ability to create order and direction in your world. The Emperor teaches that when you stand tall in your authority, life has a way of falling into place around you.

V The Hierophant – Spiritual Guidance, Tradition, and Shared Wisdom

This card is the guide of wisdom, tradition, and spiritual grounding. The Hierophant (basically a spiritual teacher with a fancy name) represents the teachings, mentors, and rituals that help us feel connected to something bigger than ourselves. He's the bridge between the earthly and the divine, offering structure not to confine you, but to support your spiritual growth. When he shows up, your spirit guides are nudging you to lean into what you already know to be true.

The best way to use this message is to reconnect to a spiritual practice or belief that steadies you. This could be meditation, journaling, pulling a card, reading something inspiring, or simply asking your spirit guides for clarity. You might also find value in seeking guidance from someone you trust or stepping into the role of teacher yourself. The Hierophant reminds you that wisdom is shared, not hoarded, and your journey expands when you let yourself learn, grow, and pass on what you've discovered.

VI The Lovers – Alignment, Meaningful Choices, and Authentic Connection

This card is the energy of alignment, connection, and meaningful choice. While it often gets labeled as strictly romantic, The Lovers is really more about harmony, both with others and within yourself. It shows up when your heart and your path want to come into agreement. When you pull this card, your spirit guides are reminding you that real connections, whether with a person, a purpose, or your own inner self, come from authenticity.

The best way to use this message is to pause and check in with your heart before you act. Move toward relationships and decisions that feel mutual, supportive, and honest. Your spirit guides want you to honor the things and people that light you up. The Lovers reminds you that when you choose from alignment, the universe responds with clarity, ease, and deeper connection.

VII The Chariot – Determination, Momentum, and Forward Movement

This card is the energy of momentum, determination, and victory through focused will. The Chariot moves forward not because the road is smooth, but because the driver knows exactly where they're headed and refuses to be thrown off course. When this card appears, your spirit guides are reminding you that you have more control than you think, and that your mix of discipline, passion, and belief is powerful enough to carry you through whatever obstacles are in your way.

The best way to use this message is to pick one goal that really matters right now and pour your energy into it without scattering yourself. Rein in distractions, tighten your focus, and trust your inner drive. Every step you take with intention builds momentum that your spirit guides can amplify. The Chariot reminds you that success comes from aligning your will with your purpose, and once you do, nothing can truly stop your forward motion.

VIII Strength – Inner Courage, Compassion, and Gentle Power

This card is the embodiment of quiet courage, compassion, and inner resilience. Strength isn't about brute force. It's about gentle power. The kind that soothes fear instead of fighting it. When you pull this card, your spirit guides are reminding you that you're stronger than the situation you're facing.

The best way to use this message is to meet whatever

challenge you're dealing with from a place of grounded calm instead of pushing, forcing, or reacting. Take a breath before responding. Offer yourself grace. Approach the problem or the person with compassion first. Your spirit guides want you to remember that resilience grows when you stay steady and kind, especially toward yourself. Strength teaches you that true power is gentle, and it transforms everything it touches.

IX The Hermit – Introspection, Soul-searching, and Inner Guidance

This card is the energy of introspection, soul-searching, and inner guidance. The Hermit steps away from the noise not to isolate himself, but to hear his truth more clearly. When this card appears, your spirit guides are encouraging you to pause, breathe, and look within.

The best way to use this message is to intentionally create a moment of solitude, even if it's small. Take a walk, sit with a journal, meditate, or simply unplug long enough to reconnect with yourself. Your spirit guides want you to honor the insights that surface when you stop rushing and get honest about what you truly want. The Hermit teaches that your inner light is reliable and wise, and when you follow it, the next step always reveals itself.

X Wheel of Fortune – Cycles, Change, and Divine Timing

This card is the heartbeat of cycles, change, and divine timing. The Wheel of Fortune reminds you that life moves in seasons with ups, downs, twists, breakthroughs, and that nothing stays static for long. When this card turns up, your spirit guides are letting you know that a shift is happening.

The energy is moving, and something in your life is ready to change. This is a moment when synchronicities increase, paths open, and momentum builds in ways you might not expect.

The best way to use this message is to stay flexible and open to opportunities as they appear. Don't cling too tightly to how you thought things had to unfold. Instead, look for the signs that things are rerouting toward something better. Say yes to the doors that crack open, even if they surprise you. Your spirit guides want you to trust the timing, trust the movement, and trust that where the wheel is taking you is exactly where you're meant to be next.

XI Justice – Truth, Balance, and Integrity

This card is the energy of truth, balance, and accountability. Justice shows up when life is asking you to look at something with clear eyes. With no denial, no excuses, just honest cause and effect. It's the reminder that your choices shape your path, and that fairness isn't about punishment but alignment. When you pull this card, your spirit guides want you to trust that doing what's right, even when it's hard, always leads you back into balance.

The best way to use this message is to examine the situation in front of you with neutrality. Ask yourself what's fair, what's honest, and what supports long-term harmony rather than short-term comfort. Make decisions that align with your values, not your fears. Your spirit guides want you to know that when you act from a place of truth, you are met with support and resolution. Justice teaches that balance is restored the moment you choose it.

XII The Hanged Man – Surrender, Patience, and New Perspective

This card is the energy of surrender, patience, and learning to see your life from a fresh angle. The Hanged Man represents that in-between space where action won't help and forcing things only closes doors. When he appears, your spirit guides are encouraging you to release the urgency, the pushing, and the pressure to figure everything out right this second.

The best way to use this message is to consciously step back and let things breathe. Instead of charging ahead, look at your situation from a different vantage point. Your spirit guides want you to trust that clarity arrives in its own timing, and that this moment of suspension isn't punishment, but is preparation. The Hanged Man teaches you that the breakthrough you're waiting for comes when you loosen your grip and allow a new perspective to settle in.

XIII Death – Transformation, Endings, and Rebirth

This card is the energy of transformation, release, and necessary endings. Despite its dramatic name, Death is not about loss. It's about clearing away what has outlived its purpose so something new can take root. It's the moment when you shed an old identity, pattern, or situation that's been weighing you down, even if part of you has been holding on out of habit or fear. When this card appears, your spirit guides are gently reminding you that endings aren't failures, they're evolution.

The best way to use this message is to acknowledge what you've outgrown and consciously release it. This might be a belief that limits you, a relationship dynamic that no longer fits, or a version of yourself you've been carrying out of obligation. Letting go creates a powerful opening. Your spirit guides want you to trust the rebirth that follows, even if you can't yet see what's coming. Death teaches you that every ending carries a new beginning in its wake, and the more willingly you make space, the faster the new energy can arrive.

XIV Temperance – Balance, Moderation, and Harmony

This card is the energy of balance and harmony. Temperance shows up when life is asking you to blend your desires, responsibilities, emotions, and intuition into something steadier and more sustainable. When this card appears, your spirit guides are reminding you that patience isn't waiting. It's trusting the process.

The best way to use this message is to moderate whatever feels extreme in your life right now. Soften the urgency. Bring your head and your heart, your work and your rest, your fear and your faith into conversation instead of conflict. Make one small adjustment that brings you closer to your center. Your spirit guides want you to know that healing and clarity happen most beautifully when you move slowly and intentionally. Temperance teaches that balance isn't a finish line. It's a practice that brings peace every time you return to it.

XV The Devil – Self-doubt, Attachment, and Reclaiming Personal Power

This card is the energy of attachment, illusion, and the inner stories that make you question your own worth. The Devil often appears when self-doubt has crept in quietly, telling you you're not enough, you can't change, or you're stuck where you are. It represents the mental loops and old patterns that shrink your confidence and make you forget your power. When The Devil shows up, your spirit guides want you to recognize that the chains holding you back are often beliefs you've outgrown but haven't realized you can set down.

The best way to use this message is to name the doubt out loud and challenge it. Then choose one small moment of self-trust today, one action that contradicts the lie your doubt is trying to tell you. Your spirit guides want you to remember that confidence returns through tiny acts of courage, not perfection. The Devil teaches that self-doubt loses its power the moment you see it as a story you're allowed to rewrite at any time.

XVI The Tower – Sudden Change, Truth Revealed, and Realignment

This card is the energy of sudden change, disruption, and the truth breaking through whatever has been built on shaky ground. The Tower isn't here to punish you, it's here to free you. It shows up when something in your life can't continue the way it has been, even if you've been trying to hold it together with hope, habit, or sheer force of will. When this card appears, your spirit guides are reminding you that breakdowns often come right before breakthroughs, especially when you've ignored the earlier nudges.

The best way to use this message is to stop clinging to what's falling apart and allow the old beliefs, relationships, plans, or identities to crumble if they need to. This is your invitation to step out of resistance and into acceptance. Your spirit guides want you to know that the aftermath of

The Tower brings clarity, fresh direction, and a more authentic foundation than you had before.

XVII The Star – Hope, Healing, and Renewed Faith

This card is the energy of healing, renewal, and gentle reconnection with hope. The Star appears after a difficult chapter (hence right after The Tower) to remind you that light always returns. When this card shows up, your spirit guides are wrapping you in reassurance, reminding you that you're on the right path even if you can't see the full horizon yet.

The best way to use this message is to lean into whatever feels soothing, authentic, and restorative. Let yourself heal at your own pace. Pay attention to small moments of inspiration, signs, synchronicities, and ideas that spark something warm in you. Those are breadcrumbs from your spirit guides. The Star teaches you that guidance doesn't always arrive as a lightning bolt. Sometimes, it's a soft glow leading you step by step toward a future that's brighter than you realized.

XVIII The Moon – Intuition, Uncertainty, and Emotional Insight

This card is the energy of intuition, emotion, and the mysteries that surface when the path ahead feels unclear. The Moon illuminates things softly, indirectly, just enough to sense, but not enough to fully grasp. When it appears, it often reflects a time of uncertainty, heightened feelings, or old fears rising from the subconscious. Your spirit guides are reminding you that your intuition is sharp right now, but your mind may be trying to fill in the blanks with worry or old stories.

The best way to use this message is to move carefully and avoid rushing big decisions until the fog lifts. Pay attention to your dreams, your gut reactions, and the subtle nudges that don't come from logic but from deep inner knowing. Let your spirit guides walk with you through the shadows. Ask for clarity, signs, or calm. The Moon teaches you that uncertainty isn't danger, it's an invitation to trust yourself more deeply. In time, what feels confusing now will become crystal clear.

XIX The Sun – Joy, Clarity, and Authentic Confidence

This card is the energy of joy, confidence, and unmistakable clarity. The Sun shows up when the fog lifts, the path brightens, and something finally clicks into place. It's the card of truth revealed in the best possible way, where everything feels lighter, clearer, and more aligned. When you pull this card, your spirit guides are reminding you that you deserve happiness without apology, and that the light you're stepping into is meant for you.

The best way to use this message is to lean into what's working and let yourself celebrate even small wins. Follow the things that energize you, the relationships that support you, and the opportunities that make you feel important. Let your confidence grow from the inside out. Your spirit guides want you to walk forward without shrinking, doubting, or dimming your glow. The Sun teaches you that life becomes clearer when you let your authentic self shine and that joy is not a luxury, but guidance all on its own.

XX Judgement – Awakening, Self-realization, and Answering the Call

This card is the energy of awakening, clarity, and stepping into a higher version of yourself. Judgment arrives when you're being called to rise above old patterns and make choices that reflect who you truly are now. It's the moment of hearing your soul's voice more clearly than the noise around you. When this card appears, your spirit guides are encouraging you to release guilt, outdated versions of yourself, and the fear of being seen as you truly are.

The best way to use this message is to reflect honestly on what your life is asking you to step into. Make space to hear that inner summons by journaling, meditating, or simply getting quiet enough to feel what resonates. Your spirit guides want you to trust the direction your soul is pointing, even if it feels bold or unfamiliar. Judgment teaches that transformation doesn't come from perfection. It comes from answering the call to become who you were always meant to be.

XXI The World – Completion, Fulfillment, and Wholeness

This card is the energy of completion, fulfillment, and integration. The World appears when a major chapter of your life has come full circle, the growth is real, and you're standing in a version of yourself that you've worked hard to become. It's a moment of accomplishment, but also of harmony. The feeling that things finally make sense. When this card shows up, your spirit guides are reminding you to acknowledge your journey, your resilience, and the wisdom you've gained along the way.

The best way to use this message is to pause and recognize how far you've come before rushing into the next beginning. Let yourself feel proud. Reflect on what this cycle taught you and how it changed you. Then, when you're ready, open yourself to the next adventure with confidence. Your spirit guides want you to know this isn't the end, but is a beautiful transition point. The World teaches that every time you reach a place of completion, you are invited to begin again from a higher, wiser place.

Tarot cards can feel magical, strange, comforting, or even a little silly depending on the day, and all of that is perfectly fine. You don't have to believe in anything mystical for these cards to help you pause, listen, and notice the messages your spirit guides are already sending. Think of tarot cards as a conversation tool, not a requirement. Use them when it feels good, set them aside when it doesn't, and let your intuition decide when it wants to pull a card.

And hey… if you made it through this chapter thinking, *Okay, that was fun, but wow, this is getting a little out there*, then brace yourself, because the next chapter is all about altars. Yes, actual spiritual spaces. Yes, I know. Yikes. But don't worry, like tarot cards, altars can be as simple, tiny, and non-mystical as you want them to be. If you're curious, join me there. If not, feel free to skip ahead. Your spirit guides won't mind either way. They simply want to connect with you, using whichever tools feel right in your hands.

19

Creating Your Sacred Space

Altars, at their simplest, are about making space. You've likely already created altar-like spaces in your life without realizing it. A candle you light when you need clarity. A meaningful object you keep nearby. A spot where you pause, even briefly, to reflect or ask for guidance. Now let's give that instinct a name and a little structure.

What Altars Are and What They're Not

Let's clear something up right away, because as we said earlier in the book, the word *altar* can carry a lot of baggage. An altar is not a religious requirement. It is not a test of how spiritual you are. It is not something you can "do wrong," and it is definitely not reserved for people who own twenty-seven crystals and know what Mercury is doing at all times. An altar is simply a physical focal point for intention and connection. That's it. No lightning bolts. No spiritual jury taking notes.

At its core, an altar is a small, deliberate space where you say (without saying a word), *this matters to me*. It's a visual and energetic anchor. A place where your attention gathers. A place where your spirit guides know, "Ah. This is where we meet." Altars don't need to be permanent. They don't need to be pretty or Instagram-worthy. They just need to be intentional. Altars are a way to signal focus to yourself and to your spirit guides. They are a way to slow down and shift out of autopilot. They are a way to create a small pause in the day where listening becomes easier than thinking. Altars work because humans are physical creatures. We respond to space, objects, and ritual.

However, altars are *not* power sources on their own. They are not magic vending machines. They are not substitutes for intuition, discernment, or action. Your spirit guides don't live *in* your altar. They don't roll their eyes if your altar is a coaster and a tea light. (If anything, they're impressed you showed up.) Think of an altar as a conversation starter, not the conversation itself. It's a place that says, "I'm open. I'm paying attention. I'm willing to listen." And honestly? That willingness matters far more than what's sitting on the table.

Choosing a Location for Your Altar

Choosing a place for your altar does not require a floor plan, feng shui certification, or permission from the universe. It requires awareness. The best location for an altar is simply a place where you will actually use it. That's the whole secret. An altar tucked away in a closet because it felt "more sacred" but never gets visited isn't doing anyone any favors. Meanwhile, a candle on a windowsill you pass ten times a day? That's an altar with a job. Start by asking yourself a few practical questions: Where do I naturally pause during my day? Where do I tend to think, reflect, or decompress? Where could I spend two quiet minutes without feeling rushed?

Common altar locations include: a bedside table or nightstand, a windowsill, a desk or shelf, a corner of a kitchen counter, or a small table or tray in a living space. None of these are more "correct" than the others. The goal is familiarity, not formality. You'll also want to consider energy and mood. Altars tend to work best in spaces that feel calm, neutral, or at least not chaotic. That doesn't mean your house has to be silent or perfectly clean. It means choosing a spot that doesn't feel constantly overstimulating. If possible, avoid places where you're always rushing past, that you associate with stress or frustration, or will be annoyed by having to move things constantly. That said, flexibility is allowed. Life happens. Altars can move. They can evolve. They can live on a tray that gets tucked away and brought back out when needed.

Privacy is another factor but not a requirement. Some people prefer a more personal space where they won't be interrupted. Others are perfectly comfortable with their altar in a shared area. There's no spiritual bonus either way. Choose what feels supportive, not what sounds impressive. Also, keep in mind that an altar that you see regularly acts as a quiet reminder. It nudges you back into awareness without effort. Even a brief glance can reset your energy or remind you to ask for guidance. And finally, trust the nudge. If a particular spot keeps catching your attention, there's probably a reason. You don't need to analyze it. You don't need to justify it. If it feels right, it is. You can always change your mind later. Your spirit guides will keep up. They're very adaptable like that.

What to Put on Your Altar and Why

Let's start with the most important rule of altars—there is no required shopping list. You do not need special tools, rare objects, or anything blessed under a full moon by someone named Ravenstar. (Unless you want that. No judgment.) An altar works because of meaning, not because of stuff. Every item on your altar serves one simple purpose, which is to help you focus, feel, or remember. If an object does none of those things, it doesn't belong there, no matter how "spiritual" it looks. That said, most altars naturally include a few common categories. Think of these as options, not obligations.

A candle. Candles are one of the simplest and most effective altar items. Lighting a candle signals the start of intentional time. It marks a transition from busy to present, from thinking to listening. The color can matter if you want it to (we covered that earlier), but a plain white candle works beautifully. Fire is about awareness, clarity, and attention. Just make sure you always use it safely.

Something that represents grounding. This could be a stone, crystal, coin, shell, or other small object from nature. Grounding items help anchor your energy in the present moment.

A symbol of connection. This is often the heart of an altar. It might be a photo, a charm, a feather, a number, a small figurine, or an object that feels quietly meaningful. This item isn't about decoration. It's about your relationship with your spirit guides and signals where they can meet you.

Optional tools. If you already use tarot cards, oracle cards, pendulums, or written questions, your altar is a natural home for them. These tools don't create guidance. They help translate it. Keep only what you actually use.

Tools that sit untouched tend to clutter energy rather than clarify it.

Just as important as what you include is what you don't. Altars are not storage spaces. They're not dumping grounds for guilt ("I should use this"). They're not places to prove anything. If an item starts to feel heavy, distracting, or stale, remove it. You're allowed to edit. In fact, editing is a form of respect.

One final tip: less is often more. A few intentional items will always be more powerful than a crowded surface. You want your eye and your attention to settle there easily. If you're ever unsure whether something belongs on your altar, ask yourself, *Does this help me feel more present, more open, or more connected?* If the answer is yes, it belongs. If not, thank it and move it along. Your altar doesn't need to impress anyone. It only needs to work for you.

Setting Up Your First Altar

This is not a ceremony. There is no right mood, no perfect time of day, and no requirement to feel "spiritual enough." This is simply an invitation to create a small space for intention. Give yourself about ten minutes. That's it.

Choose your spot. Pick a surface that feels accessible and calm. It can be anything such as a table, shelf, windowsill, or nightstand. Clear enough space to feel intentional. You don't need to deep clean. This isn't about perfection. It's about presence.

Add one anchor item. Choose one object that feels grounding or meaningful. A stone, a coin, a small keepsake, or something from nature. Place it on the surface and pause for a moment. Let this center you.

Add a candle. If you have a candle, place it near your

anchor item. If you don't, a small light or even the intention to light a candle later works. You can have more than one if you want. I use a triangle of three at a time. This represents awareness and your willingness to notice and listen.

Add one symbol of connection. Choose something that feels like a bridge between you and your spirit guides. It can be a feather, a number, a charm, a photo, or an object that carries quiet meaning. Don't overthink it. If it draws your attention, it's enough.

Set the intention. This part matters more than all the objects combined. Place your hand over the space (or simply pause and focus) and say out loud or silently something simple, such as:

"I'm open to guidance," or "I'm paying attention," or "I'm creating space to listen." Use your own words. Sincerity beats eloquence every time.

That's all there is to it. Your altar is complete. You don't need to sit with it for long. The connection builds naturally through repetition, not intensity. Over time, you may feel drawn to add or remove items. Let that happen. Altars evolve as you do. And if at any point you think, *This feels a little silly* that's okay too. Curiosity works as well as belief. You've created a doorway. You can step through it whenever you're ready.

Common Worries and Questions About Altars

"What if I don't feel anything?"

That's completely normal. Altars aren't mood switches. They're relationship builders. Some days you'll feel calm or connected. Other days you'll feel… exactly the same as before. Both are fine. Connection often shows up later, subtly, in ways you don't immediately link back to the altar.

"What if I set it up wrong?"

You didn't. There is no incorrect configuration. If your altar feels intentional and supportive, it's doing its job. Your spirit guides are not evaluating your layout choices.

"Do I have to use it every day?"

No. Altars are invitations, not obligations. Use it when you feel drawn to it. Consistency helps over time but forcing it tends to have the opposite effect.

"What if other people see it?"

That's up to you. Some people enjoy having their altar visible, while others prefer privacy. Neither choice affects your connection. If visibility makes you uncomfortable, choose a more discreet setup or a portable altar you can tuck away.

"Can I move or change my altar?"

Absolutely. In fact, it's expected. As your questions, seasons, and focus change, your altar may change too. That's not disruption. It's growth.

"What if this feels a little silly?"

That's also normal. New practices often feel awkward before they feel natural. You don't have to believe in anything special for this to work. Curiosity is plenty.

"Can I take my altar down?"

Yes. You can pause, dismantle, or restart whenever you want. Altars are tools, not commitments. You're allowed to change your mind.

Altars are meant to support you, not pressure you. If yours brings a moment of calm, focus, or intention into your day, even briefly, it's already doing something meaningful. And if all it does at first is sit there quietly, reminding you that you *meant* to listen… that counts too. An altar isn't about objects. It's about attention. It's a place where you pause long enough to say, "I'm here, and I'm listening." Sometimes that pause lasts ten minutes. Sometimes it's a glance as you walk by. Sometimes it's lighting a candle on a day when words feel hard to find. All of it counts.

Your altar doesn't need to be perfect, permanent, or profound. It only needs to feel like a place you can return to. It's a familiar doorway where connection feels a little easier and the noise quiets just enough. Here's the most important thing to remember. An altar doesn't create a connection. It helps you notice the one that's already there. As you move forward, you may find that your altar becomes less about asking and more about acknowledging. Less about searching for signs and more about recognizing them.

In the final part of this book, we'll focus on keeping that connection alive in real, everyday life. Not through perfection or constant effort, but through gratitude, trust, and small choices that support the bond you've been building all along. This is where guidance becomes sustainable, where doubt lessens, and where your relationship with your spirit guides settles into something steady, supportive, and lasting.

20

Gratitude: The Open Door to Higher Guidance

Gratitude is often treated as a finishing touch. Something you add once everything is going well. But in your relationship with spirit guides, gratitude is not the ending. It's the doorway. Gratitude keeps guidance flowing in everyday life. Not as a forced mindset or a demand for positivity, but as a simple, honest way to stay connected, especially during moments of doubt, uncertainty, or quiet. When practiced gently and consistently, gratitude becomes one of the easiest ways to strengthen intuition and recognize support as it shows up.

Why Gratitude Is the "Yes, Please" Signal

Gratitude is the simplest, most powerful way to keep guidance flowing and the best part is, it doesn't require rituals, tools, or perfect timing. It's available to you at any moment, even on the days when you feel disconnected, doubtful, or a little cranky at the world. Think of gratitude as your energetic "yes, please." It tells your spirit guides that you noticed the nudges and signs. That you are paying attention and most of all, that you would like more of that, please.

When you acknowledge what's already working, even in small ways, you're signaling openness rather than resistance. You're not begging for signs or second-guessing every nudge. You're simply saying, "Thank you." And that response matters. Spirit guides communicate most clearly when you're receptive, not tense. Gratitude opens your awareness. This doesn't mean you have to feel grateful for everything. Gratitude isn't pretending life is perfect or slapping a positive spin on hard moments. It's about acknowledging support when you see it, whether that's a clear sign, a timely thought, a moment of peace, or even simply the feeling that you didn't face something alone.

Your spirit guides respond to attention. What you notice grows and what you give thanks for tends to repeat. When you make gratitude a habit, even a quiet one, you create a steady, open channel. It's not forced. It's not dramatic. Just clear, calm, and receptive. That's why gratitude isn't only polite. It's practical. It keeps the conversation going.

A Simple Gratitude Practice to Keep Guidance Flowing

This practice takes less than a minute, but when done consistently, it can noticeably strengthen your connection with your spirit guides. Once a day, at any time that feels natural, pause and acknowledge one thing you're grateful for related to guidance or support. Just one. It doesn't need to be dramatic or life-changing. You might say (out loud or silently) something along the lines of, "Thank you for that nudge," or "Thank you for helping me notice that," or "Thank you for walking with me through this." That's it.

No follow-up request required. If you want to deepen the moment, place a hand on your heart and take one slow breath before saying thank you. This helps anchor the practice and brings your attention fully into the exchange.

On busy days, this can be even simpler. As you're brushing your teeth, getting into the car, or shutting down your computer, think or whisper, "Thank you for today." Even that little bit of gratitude counts. Some days your gratitude will be tied to something obvious. Maybe you saw a clear sign, a coincidence, or a moment of clarity. Other days it may be quieter and simply be gratitude for patience, gratitude for protection, or gratitude for support you felt but can't quite explain. All of it is valid.

If you enjoy writing things down, try this short journal prompt once or twice a week:

What did I notice today, big or small, that felt supportive, steady, or guided?

A one-sentence answer can be enough. Or write three pages if you want. You're not trying to prove anything. You're simply training yourself to notice the conversation already happening. Over time, this practice gently shifts your awareness. You stop straining for signs and start recognizing them. Gratitude becomes less about saying thank you and more about staying connected. That connection is what keeps guidance flowing.

Using Gratitude During Doubt

Doubt doesn't mean your connection is broken. It means you're human. Most people assume gratitude only works when you're feeling positive or confident, but in reality, it can be most helpful during moments of uncertainty. Not as a way to override doubt, but as a way to stay connected while you're in it. When doubt shows up, your instinct might be to stop engaging altogether. You pull back. You wait until you feel more certain, more aligned, or more "ready." But that's often when guidance feels the quietest, not because it's gone, but because your attention has turned inward toward worry. This is where gratitude becomes a lifeline rather than a celebration.

Instead of trying to feel grateful for the doubt, try expressing gratitude within it. You're not pretending everything is fine. You're simply acknowledging that support from your spirit guides doesn't disappear because clarity does. In moments of doubt, your gratitude might sound like, "Thank you for staying with me while I figure this out." This kind of gratitude doesn't require confidence. It requires honesty. You may not feel an immediate shift and that's okay. The purpose here isn't instant reassurance. It's continuity. You're keeping the line open instead of shutting it down until you feel better. Over time, using gratitude during doubt builds trust, both in the guidance you receive from your spirit guides and in your ability to navigate uncertainty without panicking. You stop interpreting doubt as failure and start recognizing it as part of the process. Guidance doesn't demand certainty. It responds to willingness. Sometimes, a simple *thank you* is the most willing thing you can offer.

How Gratitude Strengthens Intuition

Intuition doesn't usually arrive as a booming voice or a dramatic sign. Most of the time, it shows up quietly as a feeling, a pause, or a sense of this way rather than that one. The challenge isn't receiving intuition. It's recognizing it and trusting it. Gratitude helps with both. When you practice gratitude, you naturally quiet your mental noise. You move out of overthinking and into awareness. That shift makes intuitive signals easier to notice, because you're no longer scanning for proof. You're paying attention to experience.

Gratitude also builds confidence in your inner knowing. Each time you acknowledge a nudge, a feeling, or a moment of clarity and say "thank you," you reinforce the idea that your intuition is valid. You're teaching yourself to trust what you notice instead of dismissing it. Over time, this creates a feedback loop: You notice, you acknowledge, you trust, and you notice more.

It also changes how you interpret intuition. Instead of questioning whether a thought is "real" guidance from your spirit guides or only imagination, you learn to engage with it. You don't interrogate it. You listen and that listening strengthens the signal. Even when intuition turns out to be subtle or incomplete, gratitude keeps you open rather than critical. You stop judging yourself for not "getting it right" and start appreciating the process of learning your own inner language.

Intuition grows through attention, not pressure. By practicing gratitude, you give your intuition room to breathe. You create a calm, receptive space where guidance feels natural instead of forced and where trusting yourself becomes easier with time.

That's the real shift. Gratitude not only helps you hear guidance. It helps you believe yourself when you do. You might notice this in everyday moments. For example, you get a quiet nudge to take a different route home or delay sending a message. You don't know why, but you listen and later realize you avoided unnecessary stress or a conversation that wasn't ready yet. When you pause and think, *Thank you for that*, you're not simply acknowledging the outcome, you're reinforcing trust in the feeling itself. The next time a similar nudge appears, you're less likely to dismiss it or talk yourself out of it. Over time, these small acknowledgments train you to recognize your intuition faster and with less doubt, because you've already taught yourself that listening leads somewhere meaningful.

Celebrating Tiny Synchronicities

Not all guidance arrives wrapped in a big, undeniable moment. More often, it shows up as small synchronicities. Something like a word you needed overheard in passing, a song that answers a question you didn't say out loud, or a book falling into your hands at exactly the right time. These moments are easy to dismiss because they feel ordinary, but they're not insignificant. They're your spirit guides whispering instead of shouting.

When you celebrate tiny synchronicities with gratitude, you train yourself to notice guidance in real time rather than only in hindsight. A simple *thank you*, whether spoken, thought, or felt, is enough to acknowledge the connection. You're not asking for proof. You're recognizing participation. Gratitude turns these moments into anchors. Instead of thinking, *That was probably nothing*, you pause and say, "That felt meaningful." That pause matters. It strengthens awareness and builds trust in your ability to recognize support without needing dramatic confirmation.

Over time, celebrating small synchronicities changes your relationship with your spirit guides. You stop waiting for signs that feel impossible to miss and start recognizing the steady presence that's always been there. Your spirit guides don't need you to be impressed. They need you to be attentive. Tiny synchronicities aren't practice runs. They're the conversation itself. When you meet them with gratitude, you invite more of the same.

Turning Gratitude into a Ritual

Gratitude doesn't need to be formal to be meaningful but turning it into a small ritual can give it staying power. A ritual isn't about rules or performance, it's about intention. It's a way of telling yourself that this matters enough to pause. A gratitude ritual can be as simple as choosing a consistent moment in your day. Maybe it's the first sip of coffee in the morning, the moment you turn off the light at night, or the pause before you leave the house. When you pair gratitude with a repeated action, your body and mind learn to recognize it as a moment of connection.

You might place your hand on your heart and say, "Thank you." You might light a candle and acknowledge one thing that felt guided that day. You might look at an object like a coin, a stone, or a note on your altar and silently express appreciation. Over time, these small acts create a rhythm. They become a quiet signal to your spirit guides and to yourself that you're open, paying attention, and willing to listen. The ritual becomes a container for trust, especially on days when words feel clumsy or faith feels thin.

If you miss a day, nothing breaks. Rituals are invitations, not obligations. You can always begin again, because gratitude isn't something you earn. It's something you return to. When gratitude becomes a ritual, it stops being a reaction and starts becoming a relationship. And that's when guidance feels less like something you're searching for and more like something you're walking with.

A Simple Gratitude Ritual

Choose one small moment in your day that already exists. There is no need to add anything new. This ritual works best when it's tied to a habit you already have. At the same time each day, pause for a few seconds. Place your hand on your heart or abdomen and take one slow breath. Then acknowledge one thing that felt supportive, guided, or aligned that day. You might say, "Thank you for that moment at work," or "Thank you for walking with me today." When you're done, go on with your day or your night. No need to linger. The ritual isn't about staying, it's about acknowledging. Over time, this small pause becomes familiar. Comforting. A quiet check-in that reminds you that guidance isn't something you chase. It's something you notice.

Gratitude is not about being cheerful or getting everything right. It's about staying connected, especially when things feel uncertain, quiet, or unfinished. Through gratitude, you keep the conversation with your spirit guides open. You strengthen intuition without forcing it. You learn to trust small nudges and tiny synchronicities instead of waiting for undeniable proof. Over time, gratitude becomes less of a practice and more of a posture. It's more of a way of moving through the world with awareness and receptivity.

When you thank your spirit guides for what you notice, you reinforce trust on both sides of the connection. You're not asking for more before acknowledging what's already present. Gratitude doesn't demand certainty. It doesn't require perfect faith or constant clarity. It meets you where you are and walks with you forward, one moment, one nudge, or one quiet acknowledgment at a time. Sometimes, a simple thank you is enough to keep everything flowing.

As gratitude becomes part of how you move through the world, something subtle begins to happen. The connection you've been nurturing shows up not only in quiet moments, but in who you are with other people. You may feel calmer, more grounded, or more trusting of yourself, and eventually, someone notices. Gratitude doesn't just keep guidance flowing inward. It radiates outward. In the next chapter, we'll talk about what happens when the connection you've been experiencing with your spirit guides starts to ripple into your conversations, relationships, and interactions. And how to share your experiences in ways that feel authentic, grounded, and right for you.

21

Sharing the Connection with Others

At some point in your journey with your spirit guides, the experience stops feeling entirely private. You will start to notice changes in yourself. Your intuition feels sharper, your trust feels steadier, and the signs you notice feel harder to dismiss. Naturally, that raises a quiet question: *Do I talk about this with other people?*

Sharing something that feels meaningful but personal can be tricky. You may want to be open without overexplaining, honest without inviting debate, and authentic without feeling like you need to represent an entire belief system. Sharing about the connection with your spirit guides isn't about convincing anyone of anything. It's about learning how to talk about your experiences in a way that feels natural, grounded, and true to you while honoring the fact that not everyone is in the same place on their path. Whether you say a little, say nothing at all, or simply let your confidence speak for itself, there's no wrong way to do this. There's only the way that feels right for you.

What to Say to People Who Are Curious

At some point, someone in your life is going to notice something has shifted. Maybe you seem calmer, more confident, or more willing to trust your gut. Or maybe you casually mention a sign, a nudge, or a well-timed coincidence, and they pause and say, "Okay… tell me more about that." When that happens, you don't need a script. You don't need to convince anyone of anything, and you don't need to explain spirit guides in a way that feels bigger, stranger, or more dramatic than your understanding of them.

The simplest, most effective approach is to talk about your experience. Not beliefs, not theories, not cosmic rules, but simply what's been happening for you as you've started paying attention to guidance. You might say something similar to, "I've been paying more attention to my intuition," or "I've started noticing patterns that help me make decisions." Those statements are true. They're grounded. They leave room for spirit guides to be part of the picture without forcing anyone else to label it the same way you do. If they ask directly about spirit guides, it's okay to keep it light. You can describe them as a sense of support, inner guidance, or help with timing rather than something rigid or mystical. Most people aren't put off by the idea of help. They're put off by the idea of being told what to believe.

Answer questions honestly. Share what feels natural and stop when it no longer feels comfortable. You're allowed to say, "It's hard to explain, but it's been really helpful for me." That's not a cop out, it's a boundary. Some people will lean in. Some will nod politely and change the subject. Both responses are okay. Sharing the connection isn't about proving spirit guides exist. It's about letting others see what's possible when you open yourself to guidance, without dragging them there by the hand.

How to Navigate Skeptics

Not everyone you talk to will be curious. Some people will simply raise an eyebrow, while a few may be more direct in their doubt. This doesn't mean anything is wrong. It means you're encountering a different worldview. Skepticism often comes from a need to feel safe, logical, or in control. For some people, the idea of spirit guides, or any form of unseen support, feels uncomfortable because it can't be neatly measured or explained. That's not something you need to fix or fight. The most important thing to remember is this: you don't owe anyone a defense of your experience or your relationship with your spirit guides.

If someone questions what you're doing, you can keep your response simple. Statements similar to, "It's just something that's been helpful for me," or "I'm learning to trust guidance and my intuition more," are usually enough. You don't need to convince them that spirit guides are real. You don't need to win the conversation. Avoid debates. Debates turn personal experiences into positions, and once that happens, no one is really listening anymore. If the conversation starts to feel tense or draining, it's okay to gently disengage or change the subject.

It can also help to notice how you feel afterward. If you walk away doubting yourself or feeling smaller, that's a sign to share less with that person going forward. Protecting your energy is part of staying connected to your guidance and your team. And sometimes, a skeptic will quietly come back later with a question. Not in front of others. Not with fanfare. Just a soft, "Hey… can you tell me more about that thing you mentioned?" When that happens, you'll know you handled it well. Your path doesn't need approval to be valid. It only needs to feel right to you.

Sharing Signs and Stories in an Inviting Way

One of the easiest and most natural ways to talk about spirit guides is through stories. Not explanations, not definitions, but simply moments. A sign you noticed, a coincidence that made you pause, or a time when something showed up right when you needed it. Stories invite connection without pressure. They allow people to listen without feeling like they need to agree, analyze, or respond in any particular way. When you share a sign as a story, you're offering an experience, not a conclusion.

It also helps to focus on how the sign or moment made you feel rather than what you think it proves. Peace, reassurance, clarity, and comfort are universal experiences. Even someone who doesn't believe in spirit guides can understand what it feels like to be supported at the right moment. Pay attention to how the other person responds. If they ask questions or share a similar experience of their own, you can gently offer more. If they smile politely or change the subject, that's your cue to let the story stand on its own. The sign did its job whether anyone else validates it or not.

From My Experience So Far

Lately, I've been spending a lot of time talking to people about spirit guides. (That tends to happen when you write a book about them). Something interesting has become very clear to me. The responses almost always fall into three camps.

About one-third of people already get it. They're

familiar with intuition. They've noticed signs. Some of them already have language for spirit guides or a sense that there's something quietly supportive at work in their lives. These conversations feel easy and familiar, like comparing notes. When you run into these like-minded people, talking about spirit guides is fun.

Another one-third are polite but clearly not interested. They listen, they nod, and they steer the conversation elsewhere. I've been lucky and not (yet) run into anyone who is truly rude to my face about this topic. When I do, and I'm sure I will, it will be okay because I know not everyone is meant to explore this path, and no one needs to be convinced. If it happens to you, I strongly suggest you take the same high road.

Then there's that final third of people I love the most. They're curious, but cautious. Interested, but unsure. They've had experiences they can't quite explain, moments that felt meaningful or well-timed, but they don't know what to do with them. They're standing on the edge, wondering if it's coincidence, imagination, or something more, and they're not looking to be talked into anything. They're looking for reassurance. That space is where this book lives.

When you encounter these people who don't need grand claims or rigid beliefs, pause. These are the ones who simply want permission to trust what they've already been sensing. The ones who want to explore the idea of spirit guides in a way that feels safe, grounded, personal, and not overwhelming. These are the people to really talk to about what you've learned in this book and beyond. Talk to them about their curiosity. Tell them it's about paying attention. That it's about seeing what happens when you allow for the possibility that you're supported without needing to define exactly how.

A Final Reassurance

You don't need to be a spokesperson for spirit guides. You don't need the perfect words, the right timing, or a polished explanation ready to go. You don't need to educate, defend, or lead anyone anywhere. Your relationship with your spirit guides is personal. It's meant to support you first. If sharing feels natural, share. If it doesn't, don't. There will be seasons where talking about your experiences feels easy and seasons where it feels private. Both are valid. Guidance isn't measured by how visible it is.

Sometimes your role is simply to listen and quietly trust what you're being nudged toward without saying a word about it. None of that makes your connection weaker. In fact, it often makes it stronger. Your spirit guides don't need you to spread a message. They need you to stay aligned, to honor your intuition, and to protect your energy. Move through the world in a way that feels true to you. If along the way someone else feels inspired by your confidence, your calm, or your willingness to trust yourself, that's a bonus. It is not a responsibility. You are supported whether you speak about it or not. You are guided whether anyone else understands it or not. You are doing this exactly right.

As you move through the world sharing your experiences in ways that feel right for you or choosing not to share them at all, you may notice something important settling in. The need for explanation fades. The need for validation recedes. What remains is a quiet confidence in your own experience and a deep knowing that guidance isn't something you perform or prove. It's something you live with. In the final chapter, we'll take a moment to reflect on everything you've explored and gently remind you of the truth that's been present from the very beginning: you are guided. Always.

22

You Are Guided. Always

When you first opened this book, you may have been curious, hopeful, skeptical, or quietly longing for something you couldn't quite name. Maybe you were looking for answers. Maybe you were looking for reassurance that you weren't imagining the nudges, the coincidences, or the sense that there was *something more* happening behind the scenes of your everyday life.

Along the way, we explored what spirit guides are and just as importantly, what they are not. We talked about intuition, signs, symbols, repeating numbers, colors, tarot cards, altars, and gratitude. But beneath all those tools and practices was a deeper, simpler truth woven through every chapter: you are not alone, and you never have been. This journey wasn't about becoming more "spiritual" or doing things perfectly. It was about learning to notice, to listen, and to trust yourself a little more than you did before. It was to recognize that guidance often shows up quietly, in ordinary moments, through gentle encouragement rather than dramatic revelation.

If there's one thing I hope you take from everything

we've covered, it is that connection with your spirit guides isn't something you earn. It's something you remember. Once you begin paying attention, you start to realize that your spirit guides have been walking beside you the entire time.

Encouragement for Your Next Steps

As you move forward from here, know that there is no finish line you're supposed to cross and no checklist you need to complete. Your relationship with your spirit guides doesn't require perfection, constant awareness, or unwavering belief. It simply asks for openness, curiosity, and a willingness to pause and notice. Your next steps don't have to be big or dramatic. They can be as simple as asking a quiet question before you start your day. Paying attention to what keeps catching your eye. Trusting nudges. And knowing guidance often grows in the small moments, not the grand ones.

There will be days when everything feels clear and connected and days when it doesn't. Both are part of the process. Doubt doesn't mean you've lost your connection. It means you're human. Your spirit guides don't disappear when you feel uncertain. They actually tend to stand a little closer. Let yourself move at your own pace. Explore the tools that resonated with you and gently set aside the ones that didn't. This is not about following someone else's path. It's about discovering what guidance feels like *to you.* The more you trust your own experience, the more natural the conversation becomes.

A Reminder You're Never Alone

Always remember, you are never walking alone. Not on

the good days when everything seems to flow and not on the hard days when doubt, fear, or loneliness creep in uninvited. Your spirit guides don't require your constant attention to stay connected. They don't leave when you forget to ask for signs or when life gets loud and messy. Their presence is steady, patient, and unconditionally supportive. Even in moments when you feel disconnected or unsure, your spirit guides are still there quietly holding space, waiting for you to notice again.

Sometimes being guided doesn't feel mystical or obvious. Sometimes it feels similar to a calm thought in the middle of chaos. A sense of relief after making a decision. A small nudge toward rest, honesty, or self-compassion. Those moments count. They always have. When you feel lost, overwhelmed, or unsure of your next step, remember that you don't have to figure everything out on your own. You can pause. You can ask for help. You can trust that support is already woven into your life, even if you can't see all of it yet.

You have always been accompanied on this journey. The difference now is that you're aware of it. That gentle, grounded awareness is something you can return to whenever you need reassurance that you are supported, guided, and deeply cared for.

An Invitation to Re-Read, Revisit, and Deepen

This book isn't meant to be absorbed all at once and then set aside forever. Think of it as something you can return to when you need a reminder, a reset, or a little reassurance that you're still connected, even if life has pulled your attention elsewhere. You may find that certain chapters speak to you differently over time. What resonates today might shift months from now. A section that felt interesting on your first read may suddenly feel deeply personal later. That's not coincidence, it's growth. Your awareness evolves, and your relationship with guidance deepens right alongside it.

Revisit the practices that felt grounding. Re-read the stories that made you feel seen. Let yourself skip around, linger, or pause whenever something catches your attention. There is no "right" way to use this book, only the way that supports you in the moment you're in. As you continue your journey, your connection with your spirit guides will become more familiar, more intuitive, and more natural. Not because you're trying harder, but because you're trusting more. Each time you return, you strengthen that trust and deepen your own inner knowing.

Thank You for Walking and Growing with Me

Thank you for choosing to walk this path with me. Thank you for your openness, your curiosity, and your willingness to explore something that isn't always easy to put into words. Writing this book has been as much a journey for me as reading it has been for you, and knowing you were here, turning pages, pausing, and reflecting, means more than I can say. We may not share the same experiences or beliefs, but we share the same quiet questions. The same moments of doubt. The same hope that there is meaning woven into the everyday. In that way, this book is less about teaching and more about walking side by side, learning and remembering together.

If something in these pages helped you trust yourself a little more, feel a little less alone, or see your life through a clearer lens, then this book has done exactly what it was meant to do. And if you're still figuring things out? That's okay too. So am I. Growth doesn't happen all at once. It unfolds in its own time. Thank you for your trust. Thank you for your presence. And thank you for being willing to grow, listen, and notice the guidance that has always been there for you. Just as it has been there for me.

Now It's Time to Celebrate with Your Spirit Guides

Before you close this book, take a moment to pause and acknowledge what you and your spirit guides have accomplished. You showed up. You stayed curious. You allowed yourself to explore something subtle, personal, and meaningful. Your spirit guides are celebrating. Not because you read every page or tried every practice, but because you were willing to listen. Because you opened the door, even a little, and you trusted yourself enough to say, "Maybe there's more here" with an open heart.

Celebration doesn't have to be loud or elaborate (although it certainly can be). It can be quiet gratitude with a smile and a deep breath. A moment of recognition that you are supported and that you always have been. Your spirit guides don't expect perfection or constant attention. They simply enjoy being acknowledged, included, and trusted. As you move forward, carry this connection with you in whatever way feels natural. Talk to your spirit guides. Thank them. Laugh with them. Ask for help. Or simply move through your life knowing you are accompanied. This relationship is unique, evolving, and entirely your own.

So here's your invitation to mark this moment. Celebrate the awareness you've gained. Celebrate the connection you've strengthened. Celebrate the fact that you are guided. And, of course, go ahead and celebrate by high-fiving your spirit guides.

Exercises From Throughout the Book

Throughout this book, you were invited to pause, notice, and try small practices to strengthen your connection with your spirit guides. Rather than leaving those exercises scattered across chapters, they're gathered here in one place, so you don't have to hunt for them later. This section is simply a convenience. It's a way to return to the practices that resonated with you and allows you to revisit them at your own pace or try them again when your understanding has deepened.

You may notice that not every chapter included an exercise. That was intentional. Some parts of this journey are meant to be *done*, while others are meant to be understood, absorbed, or lived quietly over time. Learning to connect with your spirit guides isn't about constant action or performing every practice perfectly. It's about awareness, trust, and knowing when to engage and when to simply notice.

Use these exercises as invitations, not obligations. You don't need to complete them in order or treat them like assignments. Try one that feels right. Return to one you've already done. Skip the ones that don't call to you right now. Your spirit guides aren't keeping score. They respond to your openness, not your effort. This section exists to support you, not to add pressure. Let it be a place you come back to when you want a gentle reset, a little clarity, or a reminder that the conversation is always available.

The Gut-Check (from Chapter 1)
Instructions:

1. Don't overthink your answers. Let the first memories that come to mind be enough.
2. Write down three times in your life when you followed your gut and listened to that inner nudge.
3. Write down three times you ignored your gut and later wished you hadn't.

Key Insight to Notice:

When you followed your gut, things often worked out or you avoided trouble. When you ignored it, there was usually a cost.

A Simple Question with a Big Answer (from Chapter 2)
Instructions:

1. Take a breath and let your body relax.
2. Write down your answer to this question:
   "When in my life did I feel something was guiding me, even if I didn't know what it was?"

3. Let the first memory that comes up be enough. Don't search for the most dramatic or "spiritual" moment.

Key Insight to Notice:

The memory that surfaces first isn't random. It's an intuitive doorway you've already walked through before. Recognizing it now helps you see that guidance has been present in your life longer than you realized.

A Quick Check-In with Your Cosmic Team (from Chapter 3)

Instructions:

1. Find a comfortable spot and take a slow, relaxed breath.
2. Ask yourself quietly: *"If one of my spirit guides wanted to make themselves known right now, what is the very first feeling, image, or sensation that comes to mind?"*
3. Notice whatever appears first without analyzing or judging it.
4. Place a hand over your heart or stomach, whichever feels natural.
5. Ask one more question: *"What do I most need to hear right now?"*
6. Take the first word, phrase, feeling, or sense that arises.

Key Insight to Notice:

Spirit guides don't announce themselves dramatically. Connection usually begins with subtle awareness through small feelings, impressions, or reassurance that you might otherwise dismiss. Those quiet signals are the foundation of guidance.

A Quick Manifesting Warm-Up with Your Spirit Guides (from Chapter 3)

Instructions:

1. Sit comfortably, take one slow, deep breath, and let yourself relax.
2. Bring to mind one small, manageable desire (clarity, inspiration, or help with a task).
3. Say silently or out loud: "Spirit Guides, help me move toward this in the clearest and simplest way. Show me what I need to do and help me notice when you are guiding me."
4. Pay attention to the very next nudge, idea, or feeling that arises.
5. Write down whatever comes up, even if it feels small or anticlimactic.

Key Insight to Notice:

Manifestation with spirit guides works through small steps, not instant results. The first nudge you receive is movement and movement is how co-creation begins.

What Fear Is Actually Showing Up? (from Chapter 4)

Instructions:

1. Take a breath and place a hand over your heart or upper belly.

2. Think of one thing you're trying to call into your life right now (an opportunity, idea, decision, or deeper connection).
3. Read each of the following prompts slowly and notice which one creates the strongest physical or emotional reaction:
4. *"What if I try and it doesn't work?"* (Fear of Failure)
5. *"What if this works and I have to show up bigger than I ever have before?"* (Fear of Success)
6. *"What if this changes things in ways I can't control?"* (Fear of Change)
7. Identify which fear is most active for you right now.
8. Simply name it. Don't fix, judge, or analyze it.

Key Insight to Notice:

Naming the fear untangles it. Once you recognize what kind of fear is present, it stops muddying your energetic signal and gives your spirit guides a clearer line to work with.

The One-Sentence Request Reset (from Chapter 4)
Instructions:

1. Choose one thing you want guidance on.
2. Write your request exactly as your mind wants to phrase it. It can be messy, wordy, and over-explained.
3. Rewrite the request using only one sentence, with no explanations, caveats, "ifs," or "buts."
4. Read your one-sentence request out loud.

5. Optionally add this closing line: *"I'm willing to receive this guidance."*

Key Insight to Notice:

Clear, simple requests carry more energetic power than complicated ones. When your intention is focused and uncluttered, your guides receive a clean signal they can respond to more easily.

Spotting Your Personal Sign Language (from Chapter 5)

Instructions:

1. Think back over the last week or two.
2. Write down three moments that made you pause, even briefly (a number, object, conversation, animal encounter, or coincidence).
3. Look at the three moments and notice what feeling each one created.
4. Circle the moment that created the strongest internal reaction.
5. Finish this sentence for the circled moment: *"This got my attention because…"*

Key Insight to Notice:

Spirit guides communicate through both symbols and emotion. When you notice what stands out and how it feels, you begin distinguishing real nudges from everyday noise.

A Simple Sign-Spotting Practice (from Chapter 5)
Instructions:

1. Choose one sign category you want to focus on (numbers, animals, words, objects, etc.).
2. Set a forty-eight-hour awareness window.
3. Make a quiet agreement with your spirit guides: *"If you've been trying to reach me, I'm paying attention now."*
4. Over the next two days, notice one thing that stands out.
5. Write down what you noticed and what made it catch your attention.
6. Do not interpret or analyze yet. Simply notice.

Key Insight to Notice:

This practice trains awareness, not interpretation. Signs don't need to be dramatic to be meaningful. Noticing is the first step to clearer communication.

Spotting Your Doubt and Softening Its Grip (from Chapter 8)
Instructions:

1. Identify one area where doubt shows up most for you right now (trusting a sign, believing a nudge, or feeling connected). Write it down.
2. Ask where this doubt comes from. Is it fear, logic, upbringing, perfectionism, or old conditioning? Name the source.
3. Choose one tiny next step you can take despite the doubt. This could be trusting a recent sign,

asking for another nudge, or saying yes to something you've been hesitating about.

4. Notice how the doubt shifts after taking that small step. It may quiet or simply stop dominating your thoughts.

Key Insight to Notice:

Doubt doesn't disappear through force. It loosens when it's understood and gently moved through. Each small step teaches your mind that you are allowed to trust yourself and your guidance.

Saying Hello to Your Spirit Guide Team (from Chapter 9)

Instructions:

1. Find a quiet moment where you won't be interrupted and sit comfortably.
2. Take one slow breath to settle your body and mind.
3. In your mind or out loud, simply say "Hello."
4. Notice what happens next without searching for anything dramatic.
5. Pay attention to subtle shifts such as a change in emotion, a warm sensation, a calming feeling, a thought that appears, or a sense of presence.
6. Write down whatever you notice, even if it feels vague or uncertain.
7. If you'd like, repeat this exercise on future days to see patterns over time.

Key Insight to Notice:

Meeting your spirit guides begins with subtle awareness, not spectacle. Relationships form through small, consistent moments of connection and noticing, not instant certainty or dramatic experiences.

Writing a Conversation with Your Spirit Guides (from Chapter 10)

Instructions:

1. Write a question you want guidance on. (For example: "*What do I need to know today?*" or "*What's the next right step?*")
2. Without pausing to think, begin writing the response that comes to mind.
3. Keep writing even if it feels made up or uncertain.
4. Optional: Write your question in one color and the response in another to help separate voices.
5. Stop when the response naturally feels complete.

Key Insight to Notice:

Guidance often comes through intuition disguised as your own thoughts. Writing slows the mind enough for clearer messages to surface and helps you recognize your spirit guides' calmer, steadier "voice."

Listening Through Simple Meditation (from Chapter 10)

Instructions:

1. Sit comfortably and close your eyes.
2. Take one slow breath and allow your mind to slow down rather than go blank.
3. Sense your spirit guides nearby in whatever way feels natural.
4. Ask one simple question (for example: *"What do you want me to know right now?"*).
5. Listen for subtle shifts like new feelings, impressions, or gentle thoughts.
6. End the session after a short time, even if it's only thirty seconds.

Key Insight to Notice:

Meditation doesn't make guidance louder. It quiets your internal noise so intuitive messages have space to land.

Asking for Guidance Through Signs (from Chapter 10)

Instructions:

1. Ask a clear, specific question.
2. Choose a sign that will stand out to you (a number, symbol, phrase, animal, or song).
3. Set a reasonable timeframe (for example, forty-eight hours).
4. Go about your life without watching for the sign.

5. Notice when the sign appears and how it feels when you recognize it.

Key Insight to Notice:

Signs work best when they're intentional, specific, and emotionally recognizable. Clarity invites clearer responses.

Your First Aligned Step (from Chapter 11)
Instructions:

1. Write down one small, specific thing you want to manifest right now. Keep it simple and immediate rather than life-altering.
2. List two ways you can keep this intention in your awareness without obsessing over it (for example, a daily thank you to your spirit guides or a quiet reminder during your day).
3. Identify one tiny action you can take today that matches this intention. Choose something doable that signals readiness rather than force.

Key Insight to Notice:

Manifesting works through alignment, not pressure. When your intention, focus, and actions line up, even in small ways, your spirit guides can amplify momentum and begin meeting you halfway.

Reset & Retune (from Chapter 12)
Instructions:

1. Find a comfortable position (sitting, standing, or lying down).

2. Place a hand over your heart or stomach, wherever feels most grounding.
3. Take one slow breath in and imagine your spirit guides breathing with you.
4. As you exhale, imagine internal static clearing, like a radio tuning back into focus.
5. Close your eyes and ask: *"Where do I now feel calmer in my body?"*
6. Notice the first small point of calm and breathe into it for a few breaths.
7. Gently ask: *"What do you need me to know right now?"*
8. Allow whatever arises (an image, word, feeling, or quiet blankness) without forcing it.

Key Insight to Notice:

Connection doesn't require effort or intensity. A small moment of calm is enough to reset your energetic field and reopen the channel to guidance.

Five-Day Daily Check-In Practice (from Chapter 13)

Instructions:

1. For the next five days, choose one simple moment each morning to pause (while coffee brews, brushing your teeth, or sitting in your car).
2. Place a hand on your heart or take one slow breath.
3. Say silently or out loud, "Good morning. I'm here. Anything I should know today?"

4. Go about your day normally without searching for signs or forcing awareness.
5. At the end of each day, write down one thing that felt like guidance (a sign, a nudge, a thought, or a meaningful moment).
6. If nothing stands out, write that down too.

Key Insight to Notice:

Daily guidance builds through consistency, not intensity. Showing up in small, steady ways helps your intuition and spirit guides find a natural rhythm together.

A Simple Tool-Based Check-In (from Chapter 13)
Instructions:

1. Choose one item you feel drawn to today (a crystal, a candle, or a small spot you consider your connection corner or altar).
2. Sit comfortably and take one slow breath to settle your body.
3. Bring your attention to the item or space you chose.
4. Say a simple greeting silently or out loud, such as "Hello" or "I'm here."
5. Stay present for one or two breaths and notice any thoughts, a feeling, or nothing at all.
6. Go on with your day without trying to force meaning or messages.
7. Repeat on another day using the same tool or a different one and notice what feels most supportive.

Key Insight to Notice:

Tools don't create connections. They support it. Paying attention to what helps you feel calm, present, and open strengthens your natural intuitive channel over time.

Drilling Down to Your Real Question (from Chapter 14)

Instructions:

1. Write down a big, messy question you've been holding (for example: *"How do I fix my life?"*).
2. Ask yourself a question that narrows the focus (for example: *"What feels most off in my life right now?")* and write down the first honest answer.
3. Turn that into an even more focused question (for example: *"Should I quit my job?"*).
4. Refine it further by asking what your spirit guides can help with (for example: *"If my spirit guides could help me with one piece of this right now, what would I most want clarity on?"*).
5. Rewrite the question into a clear, specific, sign-friendly version (for example: *"Would leaving my current job in the next year support my long-term well-being and growth?"*).
6. Read the final question out loud and notice how your body responds.

Key Insight to Notice:

Clear questions create clear guidance. When your internal signal is focused and specific, signs stop conflicting and begin aligning in repeatable, recognizable ways.

Advanced Practice for When You're Ready

Up to this point, we've focused on awareness. Noticing nudges. Catching signs. Learning to trust your intuition when it taps you on the shoulder instead of hitting you over the head with a metaphorical frying pan. That alone is powerful. Many people live their entire lives ignoring those quiet inner signals, so if you've made it this far, you're already doing something meaningful. But at some point, sometimes gradually, sometimes all at once, you may feel a shift.

The signs aren't just happening *to* you anymore. They start feeling conversational and entirely intentional. As if there's a back-and-forth happening instead of a series of cosmic drive-by messages. You ask questions and get answers. You set intentions and notice movement. You start to recognize patterns not only as reassurance, but as guidance you can actively work with. That's the doorway this section opens.

I included this part of the book for readers who feel curious about what comes *after* noticing, trusting, and saying, "Okay, I think I believe this now." This practice is for when intuition becomes a relationship rather than a tool and when guidance feels less like decoding symbols and more like collaboration. That said, this is entirely optional. That's why it lives here, toward the back of the book. There's no spiritual merit badge for rushing ahead. You don't need to "graduate" into advanced practice, and nothing is broken or incomplete if you choose to stop where you are. Awareness alone can change your life in quiet, beautiful ways. Think of this section as an open door you can walk past, peek into, or come back to later. You might read it now and try nothing. You might skip it entirely and feel perfectly content.

This practice moves from recognizing signs to engaging in a full-on conversation. From trusting intuition to intentionally working with it. From hoping things line up to consciously co-creating and manifesting with your spirit guides. Not in a flashy, "control the universe" way, but in a grounded, respectful, let's-work-together way. If any of that feels like a stretch right now, that's okay. Growth isn't linear, and readiness isn't a checklist. Come here when you're curious, when things feel stable, when you want to deepen rather than fix, or when you simply feel like seeing what's possible. Nothing in this section replaces common sense, personal responsibility, or your own inner authority. If anything, it asks more of you. It doesn't require blind faith, but trust paired with discernment, and intention paired with action. Take what resonates. Leave what doesn't. Come back when it feels right. Your spirit guides will be happy with whatever you choose.

A Spoken Intention Practice for Clear Communication and Manifestation

Up to now, we've talked a lot about noticing, listening,

and responding to guidance from your spirit guides. This practice lets you take the next step: *speaking back with intention.* Words matter. Not in a fragile, "say it wrong and the universe explodes" way, but in a focused, anchoring way. When you put your intentions into clear language and then speak them aloud, especially in a calm, intentional setting, you're doing two important things at once. You're clarifying your own direction, and you're opening a clean channel for collaboration with your spirit guides.

This practice uses affirmations, but not the kind you tape to a mirror and forget about. This is a spoken declaration created by *you*, for *you*, with room for intuition and personalization. Think of it as a conversation starter. One that says, "Here's where I am, here's what I'm open to, and here's how I'd like to work together." You'll write it first. Then you'll read it aloud. That's it. No costumes required.

Step One: Write Your Intention Statement

Find a quiet place and something to write on. Don't overthink this. You're not trying to sound poetic or impressive. You're trying to sound honest. Use the prompts below to build your statement. You can write them as separate lines or blend them into a short paragraph. Follow your instincts.

Prompt 1: Ground Yourself

Right now, I am in a season of ____________________.
What feels most important to me in this moment is

____________________.

This anchors your intention in reality. Your spirit guides work best when you're clear about where you are, not where you think you *should* be.

Prompt 2: State What You're Inviting

I am seeking guidance on ____________________.
I am asking for support with ____________________.
Notice the language here. It is open, asking, and willing. You're not demanding outcomes. You're inviting collaboration.

Prompt 3: Name How You Want Guidance to Arrive

I ask that guidance comes through as ____________________.
I trust messages that arrive as ____________________.
This part is important. You're setting expectations for how communication should be delivered.

Prompt 4: Close With Gratitude

I recognize and appreciate the support that has shown up to ____________________.
I am grateful for this guidance and for the guidance already present in my life.
Never forget this part of the practice. Gratitude expresses your appreciation and gives thanks for your spirit guides.

Once you've written everything out, read it silently once. Make small edits if something feels off. When it feels right, you can set it aside.

Step Two: Prepare the Space

This is where mood helps, not because it's required, but because it signals to your nervous system that something intentional is happening. Go to your altar or a quiet space.

Light one or more candles. Choose colors that feel supportive (for this practice, I use blue for communication, white for clarity, and orange for creativity), or whatever feels right to you. There is no wrong choice here. Take a few slow breaths. Relax. You're not performing. You're arriving. If it helps, you can say something simple such as, "I'm creating space for clear, supportive communication." That's enough.

Step Three: Speak It Aloud

Take your written intention and slowly read it out loud. Don't rush. If you stumble, smile and keep going. This isn't a recital. As you read, imagine your words expanding outward, not dramatically, but steadily, similar to ripples moving across water. You're not sending out orders. You're stating truth and openness. When you're finished, pause for a moment. You don't need to wait for anything to happen. Just sit with the feeling of having been clear. You might feel calm. You might feel emotional. You might feel absolutely nothing. All of that is normal.

Step Four: Release and Return to Your Day

When you're ready, extinguish the candles. Fold the paper and place it somewhere meaningful. It can be on your altar, in a journal, or tucked into a book you love. You can return to it later or never look at it again. The power of this practice isn't in repetition (though you can repeat it). It's in clarity. You've spoken your intention. You've acknowledged partnership. You've trusted yourself enough to be direct. From here, your only job is to live your life and stay lightly attentive. Guidance often responds not with fireworks, but with timing, ideas, and small opportunities that feel strangely well-placed. That's how conversations begin. And yes, you did it exactly right.

My Example

Right now I am in a season of expansion and what feels most important to me is conveying my thoughts. I am seeking guidance on how to bring my message to the world, and I am asking for support with my writing. I am asking that guidance come through as confidence. I trust the messages that arrive as supportive signs in the form of repeating numbers. I recognize and appreciate the support that has shown up to help me with self-doubt around my writing. I am grateful for this guidance and the guidance already present in my life.

You don't need to do anything else after this. The conversation has already been opened simply because you chose to speak honestly and with intention. From here on, the guidance from your spirit guides unfolds in ordinary ways through timing, insight, clarity, and small moments of recognition that feel quietly aligned rather than dramatic. If you notice something later that makes you pause and think, *Oh… that feels connected*, trust that. If you don't notice anything at all right away, trust that too. Guidance doesn't always arrive on a schedule we can see. Often, it's weaving behind the scenes, lining things up long before we realize it.

You can return to this practice when you're at a crossroads, when something feels foggy, or when you simply want to reconnect and restate what matters to you. You can also let it be a one-time experience that did exactly what it needed to do. Both are valid. What matters most is that you spoke clearly, you listened inwardly, and you honored your own authority in the process. That combination is what deepens intuition and strengthens trust over time. Conversations don't become meaningful because they're perfect. They become meaningful because they're sincere.

Wherever this practice takes you next, know that you didn't open anything you can't handle. You didn't invite anything you aren't ready for. You simply said, "I'm here, I'm paying attention, and I'm willing to work with what comes." That is always enough.

Thank You!

Thank you for reading *High Five Your Spirit Guides*. Writing this book has meant more to me than I can easily put into words, and I'm genuinely grateful you chose to spend your time here. I hope these words stay with you long after the final page.

A Quick Favor

If you enjoyed this book, I'd truly appreciate a quick review. Reviews help other readers discover stories they'll love, and even a sentence or two makes a difference. If the book wasn't for you, that's okay too. Honest feedback helps readers make informed choices.

Stay in Touch

If you'd like to hear about new releases, behind-the-scenes moments, and reader-only updates, I'd love to have you on my newsletter.

Join here:
https://preview.mailerlite.io/forms/1981019/176588812593398843/share

I promise to keep things thoughtful, not spammy, and you can unsubscribe anytime.

About the Author

Katherine Marie writes about intuition, signs, and spiritual connection in a way that's practical, approachable, and grounded in real life. She believes guidance doesn't have to be mystical or overwhelming. It can be subtle, supportive, and woven into everyday moments.

When she's not writing, Katherine enjoys journaling, pulling tarot cards for reflection, and paying attention to the small nudges that often go unnoticed. Through her work, she encourages readers to trust themselves, stay curious, and remember they're never navigating life alone.

To stay connected and receive reader-only updates, you can join her newsletter here:

https://preview.mailerlite.io/forms/1981019/176588812593398843/share

www.ingramcontent.com/pod-product-compliance
Lightning Source LLC
LaVergne TN
LVHW010548160826
845677LV00013B/3038

* 9 7 9 8 9 9 2 1 4 3 2 1 8 *